INTRODUCTION

TO

ADVOCACY

BRIEFWRITING AND ORAL ARGUMENT
IN MOOT COURT COMPETITION

FOURTH EDITION

Prepared By

BOARD OF STUDENT ADVISERS
HARVARD LAW SCHOOL
CAMBRIDGE, MASSACHUSETTS

Mineola, New York
THE FOUNDATION PRESS, INC.
1985

Library of Congress Cataloging in Publication Data

Main entry under title:

Introduction to advocacy.

Includes index.
1. Moot courts. 2. Briefs—United States.
I. Harvard Law School. Board of Student Advisers.
KF281.A2T57 1985   808'.066347 85-10278

ISBN 0–88277–249–X

Intro. to Advocacy 4th Ed.

PREFACE TO THE FOURTH EDITION

This fourth edition of *Introduction to Advocacy* represents a significant departure from previous editions. We believe it also represents a significant improvement. The book's basic structure has not changed: it still covers research, writing, citation, and oral advocacy, the essential elements of the moot court process. Like previous editions, it includes a hypothetical case with sample briefs and record. However, we have replaced the sample case and have rewritten most of the text to make it fresher, more dynamic, and more accessible. Our changes, however, are more than cosmetic. We hope this edition reflects our conviction that there are different philosophies of litigation and thus different styles and strategies of preparing briefs and oral arguments. While the rudiments of legal research remain the same, every advocate—even the beginner—must confront important stylistic and ethical choices.

The illustrative case in this edition is *Bell-Wesley v. O'Toole*, a moot court case which has been used successfully at Harvard Law School for several years. It concerns a "wrongful birth" action brought by parents of an unplanned but perfectly healthy infant against the doctor who negligently performed a vasectomy on the husband. We think the issues are lively and current and hope that readers will find the case equally engaging. For coherence, we have illustrated points in every chapter with references to *Bell-Wesley v. O'Toole*.

The second and third editions included an appendix with articles about oral advocacy written by some of the art's most eloquent practitioners. In the interest of making the Fourth Edition more streamlined, we have eliminated the articles but incorporated ideas from them in the expanded chapter on oral advocacy. For the first time, that chapter now includes specific advice for novice oralists.

Revisions in Chapter V reflect the appearance of the 13th edition of *A Uniform System of Citation* (1981).*

Finally, an explanatory note on person and gender. Since *Introduction to Advocacy* is aimed at first year law students, we have chosen to use the second person in passages that offer particular, practical advice. We hope that addressing the reader directly will serve our goal of making this handbook useful and accessible. As far as gender is concerned, we have tried to make the text gender neutral by alternating the use of masculine and feminine pronouns in the third person singular.

* Copyright © 1981 by the Harvard Law Review Association.

ACKNOWLEDGEMENT

Introduction to Advocacy originally appeared in pamphlet form to guide first year students at Harvard Law School through the required moot court program. It metamorphosed into book form some fifteen years ago and has changed significantly since then, but not without help.

We would like to thank the members of the faculty who commented on the Third Edition and whose comments we tried to accommodate in this Fourth Edition. Professor David Shapiro and Assistant Professor Daniel Meltzer offered copious and insightful suggestions on drafts of the manuscript. Debbie Gallagher of the law school's Word Processing department provided invaluable technical support.

This book was written by a subcommittee of the Board of Student Advisers, and the members of that committee deserve high praise for their efforts: Robin Ball, Daniel Goldstein, Barbara Overton, Bob Settje, L. Anthony Sutin, Mary Lee Wolfe, and Douglas Woo contributed substantial time and energy to this project. Finally, Carol Phethean, who edited the entire manuscript and coordinated its production, merits special recognition.

BOARD OF STUDENT ADVISERS

May 1985

*

SUMMARY OF CONTENTS

	Page
PREFACE TO THE FOURTH EDITION	iii
ACKNOWLEDGEMENT	v

Chapter

		Page
I.	INTRODUCTION	1
II.	READING THE RECORD	4
III.	RESEARCHING THE BRIEF	26
IV.	WRITING THE BRIEF	37
V.	GENERAL RULES OF STYLE AND CITATION OF AUTHORITIES	98
VI.	ORAL ADVOCACY	124
Index		143

*

TABLE OF CONTENTS

Page

PREFACE TO THE FOURTH EDITION --- iii

ACKNOWLEDGEMENT--- v

Chapter

I.   **INTRODUCTION** --- 1

II. **READING THE RECORD** --------------------------------------- 4

    A. The Process-- 4

        1. Read the Entire Record ------------------------------- 4

        2. Sketch a Chronology------------------------------------ 5

        3. Narrow the Legal Issues for Appeal ---------------- 5

        4. Formulate Arguments----------------------------------- 6

        5. Connect the Factual Problems to the Legal Issues 7

        6. Develop a Core Theory -------------------------------- 8

        7. Read the Rules --- 8

        8. Read Through the Whole Record Again and Again, Until You Have a Firm Grasp of What It Contains --- 9

    B. Sample Record: *Bell-Wesley v. O'Toole* ----------------- 9

III. **RESEARCHING THE BRIEF** -------------------------------------- 26

    A. Sources Available in the Library---------------------------- 26

        1. Primary Sources-- 26

        2. General Source Tools----------------------------------- 26

            a. Secondary Sources ------------------------------- 27

            b. Bridge Sources ----------------------------------- 27

    B. The Mechanics of Legal Research--------------------------- 28

        1. General Sources -- 29

        2. Primary Sources-- 29

            a. Case Reporter/Digest Systems ---------------- 30

                (1) The West System ------------------------- 30

                    (a) Subject/Jurisdiction Determination 30

                    (b) Descriptive Word Index --------------- 30

                    (c) Case Digests------------------------------ 31

                    (d) Case Summaries------------------------- 31

                    (e) Reporters ------------------------------- 31

                  (2) The Lawyer's Cooperative System--------- 31

            b. Statutes--- 32

            c. Regulations ------------------------------------ 32

Chapter   **Page**

III. RESEARCHING THE BRIEF—Continued
                d. Case Annotated Research Tools _____ 32
                e. Shepard's Citation System _____ 33
                    (1) Locate the Proper Set of Shepard's
                          Citators_____ 33
                    (2) Look Up the Cite in the Citator _____ 34
                    (3) Check to See How Subsequent "Review-
                          ers" Have Treated the Case_____ 34
                    (4) Use the Notations to Find Supporting
                          Authority _____ 34
    C. Data Bases and Computerized Research _____ 35
    D. Tips for Researching_____ 35
    E. Conclusion _____ 36
IV. WRITING THE BRIEF_____ 37
    A. Introduction_____ 37
        1. The Purpose of the Brief_____ 37
        2. Comparing Briefwriting and Oral Advocacy_____ 37
        3. Stylistic Guidelines _____ 37
    B. The Parts of the Brief_____ 39
        1. Questions Presented _____ 39
            a. How Many?_____ 39
            b. Structure_____ 39
            c. Examples_____ 40
        2. The Introduction_____ 41
        3. The Statement of Facts _____ 41
            a. What Are Facts? _____ 41
            b. Sticking to the Record _____ 42
            c. Organizing Facts_____ 43
            d. Adverse Facts_____ 43
            e. Fact versus Argument _____ 43
        4. The Arguments _____ 44
            a. Argument Headings _____ 44
            b. Subheadings _____ 44
            c. Organization and Structure of Arguments ___ 44
            d. Rebuttal and Preemption of Arguments_____ 45
        5. The Conclusion _____ 46
    C. Use of Authority _____ 46
        1. Use of Parentheticals _____ 46
        2. Signals _____ 47
    D. Formalities _____ 47
        1. Title Page_____ 47
        2. Table of Contents_____ 48
        3. Table of Citations_____ 48

TABLE OF CONTENTS

Chapter   **Page**

IV. WRITING THE BRIEF—Continued
- E. Pitfalls to Avoid: Fact Anemia and the Agatha Christie Syndrome ... 48
- F. So You're Over the Page Limit, and Other Editing Tips ... 49
  - 1. Rewriting ... 49
  - 2. Polishing ... 49
- G. Sample Briefs: *Bell-Wesley v. O'Toole* ... 50
  - 1. Plaintiff-Appellants' Brief ... 51
  - 2. Defendant-Appellee's Brief ... 75

V. GENERAL RULES OF STYLE AND CITATION OF AUTHORITIES ... 98
- A. General Rules of Style ... 98
  - 1. Abbreviations ... 98
  - 2. Capitalization ... 99
    - a. Capitalization of Specific Words ... 99
    - b. Capitalization of Famous Old Statutes and Rules ... 99
    - c. Words Denoting Groups or Officeholders ... 99
  - 3. Italicization and Underlining ... 99
    - a. Case Names ... 100
    - b. Introductory Signals ... 100
    - c. Foreign Words and Phrases ... 100
  - 4. Numbers, Symbols, and Dates ... 100
  - 5. Quotations ... 100
    - a. Placement of Quotation Marks ... 100
    - b. Omissions From Quotations ... 100
      - (1) Short Quotations ... 101
      - (2) Clarification of Noun, Pronoun or Verb ... 101
      - (3) Omission at the Beginning of a Sentence ... 101
      - (4) Omission of the Middle of a Sentence ... 101
      - (5) Omission at the End of a Sentence ... 101
      - (6) Omission From the Middle of a Quotation ... 101
    - c. Alterations in Quotations ... 101
      - (1) Added Italics or Omitted Footnotes ... 101
      - (2) Change of Letter ... 101
      - (3) Supplementary or Explanatory Words ... 101
    - d. Page Numbers of Quoted Material ... 101
  - 6. Technical Words of Reference ... 102
    - a. *"Infra"* and *"Ibid."* ... 102
    - b. *"Supra"* ... 102
    - c. References to the Record ... 102
    - d. References to Footnotes ... 102
    - e. References to Briefs ... 102

Chapter   **Page**

V. GENERAL RULES OF STYLE AND CITATION OF AUTHORITIES—Continued

      7. The Table of Citations _____ 102

          a. Citation of Cases _____ 102

          b. Citation of Statutes _____ 102

              (1) Abbreviations _____ 102

              (2) Location _____ 103

          c. Citation of Secondary Authorities _____ 103

      8. A Note on the Spacing of Citations _____ 103

    B. Necessary Elements of Information _____ 103

      1. Identification of Authority _____ 103

      2. Where the Authority May Be Found _____ 103

      3. Indication of "Author" _____ 104

      4. Date _____ 104

      5. Indication of Purpose and Weight of the Citation 104

    C. Indication of Purpose and Weight; Order for Multiple Authorities _____ 105

      1. Signals Indicating Purpose _____ 105

          a. Authorities Supporting the Point _____ 105

              (1) [No signal] _____ 105

              (2) "*E.g.*" _____ 106

              (3) "*Accord*" _____ 106

              (4) "*See*" _____ 106

               (5) "*See also*" _____ 106

              (6) "*Cf.*" _____ 106

          b. Authorities Opposing the Point _____ 106

              (1) "*Contra*" _____ 106

              (2) "*But see*" and "*But cf.*" _____ 107

          c. Authority Not Lending Support to Proposition 107

          d. Comparing Authorities With One Another____ 107

      2. Order of Authorities _____ 107

          a. Order of Signals _____ 107

          b. Order Within Signals _____ 108

              (1) Cases _____ 108

              (2) Statutes and Constitutions _____ 109

              (3) Secondary Materials _____ 109

      3. Parentheticals Indicating Weight and Explanation 110

          a. Parentheticals Indicating Weight _____ 110

               (1) Dicta _____ 110

               (2) Concurring or Dissenting Opinion _____ 110

              (3) Points Decided by Implication; Alternative Holdings _____ 110

              (4) Plurality Opinions _____ 110

              (5) Points With Holding Unclear _____ 110

Chapter   **Page**

V. GENERAL RULES OF STYLE AND CITATION OF AUTHORITIES—Continued

      b. Explanatory Parentheticals 111
          (1) Name of Judge Writing Opinion 111
          (2) Statement of Facts 111
      c. Order of Parentheticals 111
  D. Citation of Cases 111
    1. General Rules of Form 111
      a. Parts of the Citation 111
          (1) Case Name 111
          (2) Reporter 111
          (3) Date 111
          (4) Subsequent and Prior History 111
              (a) Subsequent History 112
              (b) Prior History 112
              (c) Use of *"sub nom"* 112
      b. Omissions in Case Names 112
          (1) Secondary Parties 112
          (2) Procedural Phrases 112
          (3) Given Names and Initials 112
          (4) State Names 112
          (5) Phrases of Location 112
          (6) Consolidated Actions 113
      c. Abbreviations in Case Names 113
          (1) Commonly Abbreviated Full Names 113
          (2) Abbreviations of Words Within Names 113
          (3) Railroads 113
    2. Citations to Reporters of Federal Cases 113
      a. Supreme Court of the United States 113
          (1) If the Official Report Has Appeared 113
          (2) If the Official Report Has Not Appeared 114
      b. Lower Federal Courts 114
          (1) Federal Reporter and Federal Reporter, Second Series 114
              (a) Courts of Appeals 114
              (b) Circuit Courts 114
              (c) District Courts 114
              (d) Court of Customs and Patent Appeals 114
          (2) Federal Supplement 114
          (3) Federal Rules Decisions 115
          (4) Federal Cases 115
          (5) The Circuit Court of Appeals Reports ... 115
          (6) American Law Reports 115

Chapter   **Page**

V. GENERAL RULES OF STYLE AND CITATION OF AUTHORITIES—Continued

    c. Administrative Bodies 115

    d. Incomplete Citations 115

        (1) Where There Is No Official Citation 115

        (2) Where the Case Has Not Yet Appeared in Any Report 115

  3. Citations to Reporters of State Cases 116

    a. Official Reporters 116

        (1) Abbreviation of State Names 116

        (2) Early State Reports 116

        (3) Exceptional State Reports 116

    b. Unofficial Reporters 117

        (1) National Reporter System (West) 117

        (2) Annotated Reports System 117

    c. Incomplete Citations 118

        (1) Where There Is No Official Citation 118

        (2) Where the Case Has Not Yet Appeared in Any Report 118

 E. Citation of Statutes and Constitutions 118

  1. In General 118

    a. Session Laws and Compilations 118

        (1) Compilations 118

        (2) Session Laws 118

    b. General Rules on Form 118

  2. Federal Statutes 119

    a. General Form of Citation 119

    b. Amended Statutes 119

    c. New Statutes 119

    d. Statutes No Longer in Force and Statutes Not Appearing in Any Edition of United States Code 120

    e. Statutes Enacted by the Current Legislature 120

    f. Internal Revenue Code 120

    g. Rules of Procedure 120

  3. State Statutes 120

    a. Official Compilation 120

    b. Unofficial Compilation 120

    c. New York and California Codes 120

    d. Uniform Acts 120

  4. English Statutes 121

  5. Constitutions 121

Chapter   **Page**

V. GENERAL RULES OF STYLE AND CITATION OF AUTHORITIES—Continued

    F.   Citation to Secondary Authority 121
        1.   American Law Institute Restatements 121
        2.   Treatises 121
        3.   Law Review Articles and Notes 122
            a.   Leading Articles 122
            b.   Law Review Notes and Comments 122
        4.   Annotations 123
        5.   Additional Sources 123
            a.   Encyclopedias 123
            b.   Newspapers 123
            c.   Briefs 123

VI. ORAL ADVOCACY 124
    A.   Preparing for Oral Argument 125
        1.   Study the Record and Authorities 125
        2.   Analyze the Arguments 126
            a.   Using Your Core Theory 126
            b.   Understanding Specific Arguments 126
                (1)   Ranking the Arguments' Importance 126
                (2)   Evaluating the Arguments' Merits 127
        3.   Strategy and Style 127
        4.   Prepare Arguments for Oral Presentation 128
        5.   Anticipate Questions and Responses 129
        6.   Rehearse Your Argument 130
    B.   Organizing the Oral Argument 131
        1.   Basic Structure of Oral Argument 131
            a.   The Opening Statement 131
            b.   Statement of the Facts 132
            c.   Concise Outline of Legal Arguments 133
            d.   Making the Point 133
                (1)   Presenting Arguments 133
                (2)   Blending Fact and Law 134
            e.   Conclusion 134
        2.   The Appellee's Argument 135
        3.   Appellant's Rebuttal 135
    C.   Questions by the Court 135
        1.   The Value of Questions 135
        2.   Effective Answering 136
            a.   Be Responsive 136
            b.   Advocate 137

Chapter   **Page**

VI. ORAL ADVOCACY—Continued

      3. Particular Types of Questions Judges Might Ask 138

         a. Questions Seeking Information About the Facts _____ 138

         b. Questions About "Policy Considerations" _____ 138

         c. Questions Directed at the Authorities Cited 139

         d. Questions Directed at Particular Legal Arguments_____ 140

      4. Questioning in Team Situations _____ 140

   D. Presenting the Oral Argument_____ 140

      1. Be Yourself _____ 140

      2. Effective Delivery _____ 141

      3. What to Take to Court_____ 142

      4. Attitude Toward the Court_____ 142

      5. Handling Miscitations and Misrepresentations by Opposing Counsel _____ 142

      6. Formal Conduct_____ 142

Index _____ 143

INTRODUCTION

TO

ADVOCACY

BRIEFWRITING AND ORAL ARGUMENT
IN MOOT COURT COMPETITION

*

Chapter I

INTRODUCTION

Having first year law students develop their skills at writing briefs and delivering an oral argument in a moot court setting is a long standing tradition, even though many lawyers never find themselves in a courtroom. Participating in a required moot court exercise may seem to have no relevance for the student who aspires to be a corporate wheeler-dealer or a scholarly tax professor, yet taking a case through every stage of the appellate process is useful for many reasons.

The skills needed to perform expertly in moot court competition—research, writing, and speaking—are essential for an attorney in any area of practice. Writing a brief for moot court develops a student's ability to formulate persuasive arguments, write convincingly, and support assertions with well-researched authority. Because lawyers constantly find themselves on the phone or in conference rooms with clients and other attorneys, the ability to think on one's feet, answer questions under pressure, explain complex issues clearly, and at the same time maintain an air of mastery and confidence is an important practical skill for which oral argument is an excellent preparation.

The typical model for a law school's moot court program is an appellate case. Traditionally, moot court programs were competitive. In recent years, many law schools have eliminated the competitive aspect of their first year moot court programs in order to shift the emphasis from winning to learning and skill development. Whether or not your own moot court program is an actual competition, you should remember that the most important thing about participating is how much you can learn about lawyering and how much you can improve your writing and speaking abilities.

This book has three broad, interrelated goals: 1) to describe how to accomplish every stage of a moot court exercise, starting with interpreting the paper record and moving through oral argument; 2) to illustrate the narrative descriptions with specific examples; and 3) to serve as a resource that students can refer to at any point during the program—while trying to develop a research strategy and write the brief, while typing a citation or table of contents, or while preparing for the new experience of oral argument.

The book's structure reflects these goals. Each chapter that follows covers a discrete topic: Reading the Record; Researching the Brief; Writing the Brief; Citation; and Oral Argument. Examples and illustrations in every chapter are drawn from *Bell-Wesley v. O'Toole,* a hypothetical "wrongful birth" suit brought by parents of an unplanned child against the doctor who negligently performed the husband's vasectomy. The full moot court record appears at p. 11; sample briefs for both the appellants and the appellee are at p. 51, immediately following the chapter on briefwriting.[1] Finally, the detailed index and table of contents are intended to facilitate the use of *Introduction to Advocacy* as a reference.

This book is about moot courts, not real courts. Much of what it has to say about briefwriting and oral argument is applicable to appellate litigation in general, but readers should always keep in mind that moot court has characteristics that distinguish it from appellate practice in the real world. For example, moot court judges—frequently law school professors or upperclass students—often scrutinize the briefs prior to argument and are perhaps more likely to quiz an oralist on her knowledge of specific cases. They may ask scholarly, less practical questions than those that federal or state judges might pose. Frequently, moot court judges will discuss an oralist's performance with her after the argument in order to point out strengths and offer suggestions on how to improve weaknesses. Real judges do not take the time to tutor the attorneys who come before them. Many moot court cases are argued in mythical jurisdictions where no precedent controls but all precedents may have some persuasive value. Real cases arise in places where particular statutes and case law not only apply but are binding. Finally, in some moot court programs students work in teams of four, with two students representing appellants and two representing appellees. The four team members collaborate on research and preparation throughout the exercise. When it comes time to argue the case, the pairs split up and argue against students on another team. This approach enables each side to see the strengths and weaknesses of its position and learn how an opponent would characterize the same facts from a contrary perspective. This symmetric collaboration does not exist in the "real world."

Despite the differences, there are many similarities. As in real courts, moot court rules set limits on the length of briefs and oral arguments. Moot court participants are constrained by the contents of the hypothetical trial record in the same way that appellate lawyers are. Moot court arguments are often heard by a panel of judges, as they are in federal and state appellate courts.

Throughout the process of building an effective appellate case, you will be called upon to make strategic and stylistic choices

---

[1] These briefs reflect ideas and approaches used by many first year students who researched and argued *Bell-* *Wesley v. O'Toole* in the moot court program at Harvard Law School.

concerning the nature and presentation of your arguments. There are many ways to practice the art of advocacy—probably as many ways as there are lawyers. This book attempts to present the technical framework upon which you can build an effective and unique argument—*your* argument. Examples in each chapter emphasize the many ways one can make the substantive points, each way conveying a different sense of overall strategy and style. Keep in mind as you read this book and as you develop your case that the arguments you devise are not merely the products of the technical requirements of lawyering but are also a reflection of your personality and the strength of your creative and legal insight.

Chapter II

READING THE RECORD

In appellate moot court competition, as in real life appeals, the record is the lawyer's sole source of information about the facts of the case. The record for the appeal compiles all the legal and factual determinations made by the lower court and includes the various pleadings and motions the parties filed in the lower court, as well as the trial transcript, affidavits of various witnesses, and the lower court opinion. In a moot court record the various documents usually appear in an abbreviated form. An actual record can be thousands of pages; the usual moot court record will be much shorter. The sample record in *Bell-Wesley v. O'Toole*, which follows this chapter, is a typical example.

Read the record closely and carefully in order to discover the factual and legal issues presented in the lower court. Your job on appeal is to examine the lower court opinion closely to determine the precise legal grounds for the opinion, the potential issues of reversible error, and the available arguments for your position. Because the record is your only source of factual information, a clear understanding of the record is prerequisite to an effective appeal.

A. THE PROCESS

There is no single way to read and understand the record. Each person needs to determine what method is best for him. One possible approach is as follows:

1. Read the entire record.
2. Sketch a chronology of what happened.
3. Narrow the legal issues for appeal.
4. Formulate arguments.
5. Connect the factual problems to the legal issues.
6. Develop a core theory.
7. Read the rules.
8. Read through the whole record again and again, until you have a firm grasp of what it contains.

1. Read the Entire Record. Before trying to distill and narrow the information available to you in the record, you must have a broad overview of the case. A first read-through, even a fairly quick one, will help you understand what is happening both legally and factually. With a broad overview, you can begin to narrow the legal and factual problems for the appeal.

2. Sketch a Chronology. The items in a record are not necessarily arranged in the order in which events actually happened. By writing out a chronology of events, you will have a comprehensive and detailed understanding of the factual setting. This is important because many cases turn on not what happened but when it happened.

For example, in *Bell-Wesley v. O'Toole,* one of the important issues in determining whether damages should be awarded is whether Frank's birth harmed Rebecca Bell-Wesley's career goals. You need to look at the trial record of Rebecca's testimony to learn about her potential lost career opportunities. A reading of the record shows that Rebecca became pregnant after she accepted a new position at the attorney general's office. This is very important because if Rebecca had become pregnant before she accepted the new position, she would be unable to claim damages.

In ordering the facts, you will also discover what facts you do not have. In any court record, moot or otherwise, some facts will be missing or ambiguous. Once you notice what facts are missing, look more closely at the record to see if these facts are hidden or if they can be reasonably inferred from available facts. Facts inferred from the record should become a part of your argument and may be introduced in the Statement of Facts. If you choose to include them in the Statement of Facts, be sure to preface them in a way that signals to the court that you are making an inference. Remember that the only undisputed facts are those in the record. Nothing will defeat your credibility with a court more than the misuse of facts or the use of inference as undisputed fact.

As you read the record, be aware of the importance that the court will attach to the source of a fact in assessing its weight. For example, most records in a civil trial will contain the original complaint and answer. These contain the facts as presented by the parties and not as determined by the court. In *Bell-Wesley v. O'Toole,* the court made specific findings of fact that would be accorded significantly more weight by an appellate court than the allegations present in the complaint or answer. However, allegations in the complaint admitted in the answer are considered indisputable facts. But asserting unadmitted allegations in the complaint as indisputably true presents the court with a distorted version of the factual setting.

3. Narrow the Legal Issues for Appeal. At the lower court level, many issues are decided. On appeal, however, the legal issues are normally narrower and more defined. Determine which of the lower court's decisions are at issue on appeal so that you concentrate only on relevant facts and issues. Sometimes the court will limit the issues for you, as on the last page of the *Bell-Wesley v. O'Toole* record. (See p. 25.) After reading this, you know that you need not consider the possible negligence arguments concerning the vasectomy.

Probably the best place to discover the relevant legal issues on appeal is the lower court opinion. It discusses the reasons for the court's ruling and should frame the issues for appeal. Here, Judge Llewenstein's fifth and sixth conclusions of law point you to the two vital issues on appeal: can there be damages for a "wrongful birth," and what items should enter into the calculation of these damages. (See p. 19.) In other cases, the opinion and record will not so clearly frame the issues, but a careful reading of the opinion and other documents should provide you with the important legal issues for the appeal.

In narrowing the issues for appeal, focus on policy, legal, and factual questions raised by the record. *Bell-Wesley v. O'Toole* presents such policy questions as:

(1) Should society allow parents, who wish to keep their child, to force the doctor who negligently performed a vasectomy to pay for all of the costs that parents would normally incur in raising a child?

(2) What impact would that have on a child?

(3) On the medical profession?

(4) Would a decision against the doctor make it more difficult to find another doctor willing to perform a sterilization procedure?

The case also presents factual questions. For example:

Were the parents actually traumatized by the birth, when in fact they had attempted to have children before opting for sterilization?

You need not, and probably cannot, determine all of the issues presented by the case before beginning to research. Indeed, in the course of library research you should continuously be refining issues and discovering new ways of looking at the case. Legal research is a dynamic process of moving from defining issues to developing arguments to finding support and then back again. Issues and arguments will inevitably be reformulated as you discover the content of statutes and case law.

4. Formulate Arguments. The arguments you make in your written and oral presentation to the court answer the questions raised by the issues in your case. These arguments provide the reasons the court should find in your favor when resolving these issues.

Formulating arguments is a dynamic process, involving reason and analysis as well as reliance on authority. Before you go to the library to see how others have answered these questions, try to generate a list of answers yourself. Don't be afraid to rely on your intuition at first. Begin thinking of how you can best frame the arguments for (and against) the position that you wish to support. This list of sources will help generate some ideas:

(a) Arguments based on commonsense notions of justice and equity—often one's client got into a predicament through a good-faith belief about the correctness of a certain action;

(b) Arguments based on authorities and case law that you have already studied;

(c) Arguments by analogy or comparison to other cases and situations with which you are familiar;

(d) Arguments from the nature of the subject matter of the case;

(e) Arguments based on the potential consequences of the court's finding or not finding your way;

(f) Arguments stemming from personal concerns;

(g) Arguments affecting public policy, i.e., society's concerns about the issues presented.

This list is a starting point for research. During the course of your research you will of course discover new arguments to add to the list and reject some arguments as frivolous.

5. Connect the Factual Problems to the Legal Issues. By now, you have a solid grasp of what actually happened and a basic understanding of the legal considerations. You must now synthesize the two sets of information. As will be discussed in Chapter IV, Writing the Brief, and Chapter VI, Oral Advocacy, the key to an effective argument will be your ability to relate the legal arguments to the specific factual situation.

This requires you to look critically at the information the record gives to determine which facts matter the most to your arguments. In this case, not every fact concerning Dr. O'Toole's performance of the vasectomy matters. Important facts are those that demonstrate how the wrongful birth of a child can be a real injury to the parents. Examples of the economic and emotional cost to Rebecca and Scott Bell-Wesley can be used for this purpose.

The process of relating the facts to the law helps you continually redefine the factual and legal issues. By evaluating the relationship between the two, you will begin to analyze critically both your factual and legal determinations. Your understanding of both areas will improve in the process.

6. Develop a Core Theory. After generating a series of useful arguments, try to combine their essences into a single coherent thought, or "core theory." Library work will be necessary before the theory crystallizes, but you should begin to formulate this theory before beginning your research.

The core theory presents the foundation of your position. It should be based on and reflect a knowledge of all the factual and legal issues of your case. It ought to convey the central argument of your case, so that you can rely on it in your brief and in oral argument. It should be logical and persuasive, simple and memorable, clear and appropriate.

Finding your core theory takes time and thought. Throughout your work, think about the arguments you generate from the record and your research. Try to distill your ideas into a theory that captures the heart of your case in a few words or sentences. The strand that connects your ideas into a cohesive whole is your core theory.

Here are some examples of what a core theory could look like for the appellant and appellee in *Bell-Wesley v. O'Toole:*

Appellant:

Rebecca and Scott Bell-Wesley's wrongful birth claim is indistinguishable from any other medical malpractice claim. They must be compensated for all of the injuries flowing from Dr. O'Toole's repeated negligence and the resulting birth of a child after they had chosen to lead a childless lifestyle.

Appellee:

The Bell-Wesleys should not be awarded damages to pay for the costs of raising their son because they wanted a healthy child. They were not injured by his birth.

Be aware that any case can give rise to a number of alternative core theories. For example, another appellant's core theory might have been:

The Bell-Wesleys should be compensated for the costs of raising a child which they chose not to have and, but for the doctor's negligence in performing Scott Bell-Wesley's vasectomy, would not have had because their right to determine the size of their own family has been infringed.

7. Read the Rules. This is often a good time to familiarize yourself with the rules of your particular court, be it moot or authentic. Doing so now will avoid unnecessary rude shocks further down the line. The rules will supply information about deadlines and page limits, as well as format. Follow them carefully. While these guidelines are usually included with moot court documents, you should be aware that "real" rules are contained both in national compilations, such as the Federal Rules of Appellate Procedure, and local or circuit rules.

8. Read Through the Whole Record Again and Again, Until You Have a Firm Grasp Of What It Contains. This is probably the most tedious step in the process, but its importance cannot be overemphasized. The more times you read through the record, the better your understanding of the facts will be. You may discover inconsistencies and omissions in the record as you become more and more familiar with it. The better you understand these problems, the better your ability will be to confront them.

It is tempting to skip the determination of issues and arguments and head straight to the library. The time-savings of doing this are only illusory. You are headed into uncharted territory and without a road map you will probably find yourself exploring many unproductive paths. You should always feel free to adopt arguments you discover during research, and not feel compelled to hold on to an untenable albeit creative argument that you generated during a pre-research brainstorming session. However, the best ideas are often generated in a brainstorming session before visiting the library. Think before you begin searching.

B. SAMPLE RECORD: BELL–WESLEY v. O'TOOLE

The sample moot court record for *Bell-Wesley v. O'Toole* appears on the following pages. Examine it carefully to see what documents it includes and what factual and legal issues it raises. Note especially that instructions on the last page limit the issues available to moot court participants; for example, whether the doctor's performance of the sterilization operation was negligent is not an issue. This type of constraint is common in moot court programs where skill development is more important than an exhaustive consideration of all possible issues.

Once you are familiar with the *Bell-Wesley v. O'Toole* record, you may want to compare your understanding of the facts and legal issues with the questions presented and the statements of the case in the sample briefs following Chapter IV.

*

COMPLAINT

SUPERIOR COURT FOR THE STATE OF AMES

REBECCA AND SCOTT BELL-WESLEY, Plaintiffs	)	
	)	
v.	)	CIVIL ACTION 83-2004
	)	
	)	COMPLAINT
DR. STEPHEN O'TOOLE, Defendant.	)	

JURISDICTION

1. Plaintiffs Rebecca and Scott Bell-Wesley are a married couple residing in the state of Ames.

2. Defendant Stephen O'Toole is a medical doctor who resides and has his medical office in the state of Ames.

CAUSES OF ACTION

3. Plaintiff Scott Bell-Wesley is an architect, under employment of the city of Holmes, City Planning Department.

4. Plaintiff Rebecca Bell-Wesley is an attorney, practicing with the state of Ames's Attorney General's office, in the city of Holmes.

5. Prior to January 4, 1983, plaintiff Rebecca Bell-Wesley had given birth to three deformed children, each of whom had died within six months after birth. Defendant O'Toole informed plaintiffs that there was a 75% chance that any child they conceived would suffer and die from the same congenital deformity.

6. Plaintiffs chose to lead a childless lifestyle by procuring a sterilization operation.

7. On October 16, 1981, defendant performed a vasectomy on plaintiff Scott Bell-Wesley for the purpose of preventing conception and birth of a child.

8. Defendant O'Toole was solely responsible for the performance of said operation, and for plaintiff's post-operative case.

9. Plaintiffs were advised by defendant that the operation would not render him sterile immediately, and that an alternative means of birth control should be used by plaintiffs until ten (10) weeks after the operation.

2

10. Plaintiffs used an alternate method of birth control for 3 months after Scott Bell-Wesley's vasectomy.

11. Plaintiffs were further informed by defendant O'Toole that a sperm count would have to be performed 12-14 weeks after the operation in order to determine the success of the operation.

12. Plaintiff Scott Bell-Wesley returned to the office of defendant O'Toole on January 8, 1982, at which time the defendant performed a sperm count and informed the plaintiff that he was sterile.

13. Plaintiff Rebecca Bell-Wesley was found to be pregnant on April 20, 1982 by defendant O'Toole.

14. Plaintiff Rebecca Bell-Wesley gave birth to Frank Michael Bell on January 4, 1983.

15. Plaintiff Scott Bell-Wesley is the biological father of Frank Michael Bell.

16. Defendant's separate acts of negligence were the proximate causes of the injury suffered by plaintiffs.

17. Plaintiffs were injured by the birth of their unplanned child.

18. Defendant's negligence has denied plaintiffs of their constitutionally protected right of self-determination in matters of childbearing.

19. Plaintiffs have incurred mental, physical, and financial injuries as a result of the conception and birth of their child, for which defendant is liable.

REMEDY

Wherefore, plaintiffs pray the court for the following relief:

20. That defendant be held liable to plaintiffs for the cost of Scott Bell-Wesley's vasectomy, including his medical expenses, his pain and suffering, and Rebecca's loss of consortium during his recuperation period in the amount of $1500.

20. That defendant be held liable to plaintiffs for the medical expenses and pain and suffering caused by Rebecca Bell-Wesley's pregnancy and for Scott Bell-Wesley's loss of consortium during the last part of her pregnancy in the amount of $3,000.

22. That the defendant be held liable to plaintiff Rebecca Bell-Wesley for the medical expenses and pain and suffering

3

caused by her giving birth to Frank Michael Bell, in the amount of $5,000.

23. That defendant be held liable to plaintiffs for their emotional trauma caused by the conception and birth of an unplanned and unwanted child and for the additional emotional trauma resulting from plaintiffs' reasonable expectation that the child would suffer from a congenital deformity, in the amount of $10,000.

24. That the defendant be held liable to plaintiffs for lost earnings incurred as a result of Rebecca Bell-Wesley's pregnancy, and the birth and care of their child in the amount of $20,000 (see Trial Record, attached).

25. That the defendant be held liable to plaintiffs for injury to their lifestyle, which is impacted in many ways by the care and rearing of their child, and for their loss of control over their leisure hours, in the amount of $50,000.

26. That the defendant be held liable to plaintiffs for the financial and emotional cost of rearing their child, in the amount of $50,000 (see Exhibit B attached).

Plaintiffs further pray that the court order any additional measure of damages as would be just, and that provision for attorney's fees be made.

Respectfully submitted,

Scott and Rebecca Bell-Wesley
by their attorney

Jane E. Harvey
Llewellyn, Murray & Silber
325 North Bridge Road
Holmes, Ames

4

Exhibit A (in part)

From the 1982 annual report by the Dept. of Health and
Human Services, Washington, D.C.

The cost of raising a child, outside of possibly purchasing
a home, is the single greatest investment a family will
make. Current projections, stipulating that there is virtually
no limit on what a couple may invest, indicate that the very
minimum parents will spend bringing a child up to majority
will be $50,000. This figure includes the basic costs of
housing, feeding, and clothing the child, as well as the
minimum costs of maintaining his/her health up to age eighteen.
Addition of even several moderately priced "extras"--early
professional child care, private schooling, college, allowances
for serious illness--can push the cost of childrearing
beyond $100,000. And these figures do not yet even contemplate
the emotional costs of raising a child. . . .

5

SUPERIOR COURT FOR THE STATE OF AMES

REBECCA AND SCOTT BELL-WESLEY,)
             Plaintiffs,)
)
           v.   )   CIVIL ACTION 83-2004
)
DR. STEPHEN O'TOOLE,   )   DEFENDANT'S ANSWER
             Defendant.)

1. Defendant admits the allegations in paragraphs 1-5 of plaintiffs' complaint.

2. Defendant denies the allegations in paragraph 6 of plaintiffs' complaint.

3. Defendant admits the allegations in paragraphs 7-14 of plaintiff's complaint.

4. Defendant is without sufficient information to respond to paragraph 15 of plaintiffs' complaint.

5. Defendant denies the allegations in paragraphs 16-26 of plaintiff's complaint.

FIRST AFFIRMATIVE DEFENSE

6. Plaintiffs assumed the risk of possible failure of the sterilization procedure.

7. Since even perfectly performed vasectomies are not successful in all cases (statistical rate of regrowth of the tubes) plaintiffs have assumed the risk of failure of the operation whether resulting from negligence or regrowth.

8. Since the social value of sterilization operations is so high, society has imposed this "assumption of risk" or waiver of recovery rights for those engaging in a procedure which cannot yet be made 100% effective, regardless of whether negligence was involved.

SECOND AFFIRMATIVE DEFENSE

9. Defendant was not negligent in his operative or post-operative procedures with plaintiff Scott Bell-Wesley.

10. Plaintiff Scott Bell-Wesley suffered a tubal regrowth which was a statistical failure of the procedure, not caused by defendant's negligence.

6

THIRD AFFIRMATIVE DEFENSE

11.   The birth of a child is always a benefit and a blessing which outweighs any financial costs, as well as any pain and suffering incurred during pregnancy.

12.   Where the parents' express purpose in procuring a vasectomy was to prevent the birth of a deformed child, the birth to the parents of a healthy child causes them no injury.

13.   Therefore the plaintiffs did not suffer any damages and defendant is not liable to plaintiffs.

FOURTH AFFIRMATIVE DEFENSE

14.   Broad social policies prohibit the awarding of damages in actions for wrongful birth.

15.   Therefore, plaintiffs have failed to state a cause of action for which relief can be granted.

FIFTH AFFIRMATIVE DEFENSE

16.   Plaintiffs have failed to mitigate the damages they suffered, by choosing not to terminate Rebecca Bell-Wesley's pregnancy by abortion.

17.   Plaintiffs have additionally failed to mitigate the damages claimed in paragraph 23 of their complaint by refusing, as they have in the past, to undergo amniocentesis, a safe, simple test conducted early in the pregnancy which would have determined that child being carried was, and is, normal and healthy.

18.   Plaintiffs have further failed to mitigate the damages in that they have not offered their "unwanted, unplanned" child up for adoption.

Respectfully submitted,

Dr. Stephen O'Toole
by his attorney

D. Nathan Neuville
Ericson, Swanson and Moses
1977 Pond Ave.
Holmes, Ames

7

SUPERIOR COURT FOR THE STATE OF AMES

REBECCA AND SCOTT BELL-WESLEY,)
        Plaintiffs,)
)
)
          v.   )   CIVIL ACTION 83-2004
)
DR. STEPHEN O'TOOLE,   )   FINDINGS OF FACT AND
        Defendant.   )   CONCLUSIONS OF LAW

FINDINGS OF FACT

1. Plaintiffs made a conscious decision to avoid the possibility of the conception and birth of a child. The motive for this decision was their fear of having another deformed child.

2. In furtherance of this decision, Scott Bell-Wesley obtained a vasectomy from Dr. O'Toole on October 16, 1981.

3. Expert testimony showed that defendant failed to properly sever the tubes of the vas deferens, and the plaintiff was never rendered sterile.

4. Defendant negligently performed a sperm count and informed plaintiff Scott Bell-Wesley that he had been rendered sterile.

5. Defendant is a general practitioner medical doctor who has performed vasectomies in his office over the past few years.

6. Plaintiff Rebecca Bell-Wesley conceived and bore a child, Frank Michael Bell, on January 4, 1983.

7. Scott Bell-Wesley has been established to be the biological father. The pregnancy and childbirth were normal and without complications, except that they were unplanned; Frank Michael Bell was born healthy and has remained so since.

8. Plaintiffs declined to abort the child on moral grounds, and have declined to give the child up for adoption for various personal reasons.

9. Plaintiffs' lifestyle has changed dramatically since birth of the child.

10. Both parents have lost, and will continue to lose, time and wages in their chosen careers as a result of caring for the child.

8

11.   Both parents profess a deep love for their child even though they bring the present action.

12.   Expert testimony established that amniocentesis would have revealed that the fetus was not deformed and was in fact in good health.

9

CONCLUSIONS OF LAW

1. Defendant Dr. Stephen O'Toole performed a vasectomy on plaintiff Scott Bell-Wesley on October 16, 1981 which was unsuccessful.

2. Defendant O'Toole negligently performed a sperm count and informed plaintiff Scott Bell-Wesley that the operation was successful and he had been rendered sterile.

3. The conception and birth of plaintiffs' child would not have resulted had the operation been successful.

4. Plaintiffs have stated a cause of action for negligence.

5. Plaintiffs' damages are limited to the out of pocket costs, pain and suffering, and loss of consortium associated with Scott Bell-Wesley's vasectomy. A reasonable award for these damages is $500.00.

6. Damages are not awardable for the costs associated with pregnancy, birth, and rearing of a healthy child because the benefits of a healthy child always outweigh any attendant costs.

DATED: May 13, 1983   Signed

                               _____

                               NANCY LLEWENSTEIN

                               Ames Superior Court Judge

10

SUPERIOR COURT OPINION

Llewenstein, J.

In this bench trial, we are faced with a difficult problem involving not only the rights of individuals, but also numerous social and systemic considerations as well. It is apparent to us that the operation was performed negligently. Not only was the operation itself ineffective, but the defendant was subsequently negligent in performing a sperm count on the plaintiff and in informing him, on the basis of this test, that he had been rendered sterile.

Yet plaintiffs allege that the birth of a healthy son must somehow be compensated by the defendant. The idea that a child would grow up being supported by another by virtue of the fact that his parents did not plan for or want him is, to us, repulsive. The very real inability to assign a dollar amount to such an "injury" is exceeded only by the harm which such an award could do to families and individuals in our society. Perhaps we are old-fashioned, but we are still filled with mystery, joy and inspiration at the birth of a new human life. In this case, where the plaintiffs' prior conceptions resulted in the birth and tragic deaths of three congenitally deformed infants, the birth to them of a healthy child is truly a blessing. The benefits of a healthy child clearly outweigh any and all associated costs, even those attributed to the unplanned pregnancy.

Scott Bell-Wesley's vasectomy was improperly performed and the post-operative care he received was inadequate. The defendant is liable for his improper medical treatment, and therefore damages of $500.00 are awarded to plaintiffs. However, we in Ames decline to join the ranks of jurisdictions recognizing a cause of action for wrongful birth. The benefits of a healthy child always outweigh any attendant costs or burdens. This case is no different.

11

Trial Record

(Parts have been omitted)

Counsel: Mrs. Bell-Wesley, what happened in the months
following the presumably successful sterilization
procedure?

Rebecca Bell-Wesley: Well, shortly after Scott's vasectomy
I accepted an offer from the Attorney General to
become one of his first assistant attorneys general.

Counsel: Are there many of these First Assistant Attorneys
General?

R.B.-W.: Oh, no. Just a handful--no more than four or
five, each located in a different city in Ames.

C: I see, and there is more involved in this than in
your prior position?

R.B.-W.: Yes, various department heads reported to me. I
also had considerable discretion over the policies
to be promulgated by our office as well as identifying
the goals sought through our litigation and authorizing
compromises and settlements.

C: You say had. Are you no longer in this position?

R.B.-W.: It's not clear. I have taken a six month leave of
absence, so I should return to work sometime in
May. In the meantime, many things could happen.
The Attorney General's is a political office, you
know.

C: And your position as Assistant Attorney General
was politically obtained?

R.B.-W.: No, the Attorney General usually only bothers
himself with hiring or bringing in his own first
assistants and department chiefs. I was hired out
of law school by a department chief at the time.

C: And what was your salary change upon acceptance of
your most recent position?

R.B.-W.: I went from $24,000/yr. to $40,000.

12

SUPERIOR COURT FOR THE STATE OF AMES

REBECCA AND SCOTT BELL-WESLEY,)
        Plaintiffs,   )
)
         v.   )   CIVIL ACTION 83-2004
)
DR. STEPHEN O'TOOLE,   )   JUDGMENT
        Defendant.   )

(JUDGMENT OF TRIAL COURT)

   The issues in the above action having duly been heard by
this court, and this court having made and filed its findings
of fact and conclusions of law on May 13, 1983, it is,
therefore,

   ORDERED, ADJUDGED, AND DECREED, that judgment be entered
for plaintiffs as to Defendant's acts of negligence and
plaintiffs be awarded $500.00 in damages.

DATED: May 20, 1983   Signed

                                _____
                                  Clerk of Court

13

SUPERIOR COURT FOR THE STATE OF AMES

REBECCA AND SCOTT BELL-WESLEY,)
                  Plaintiffs,)
)   CIVIL ACTION 83-2004
            v.   )
)   NOTICE OF APPEAL
DR. STEPHEN O'TOOLE,)
                 Defendant.)

  Notice is hereby given that Petitioners, Rebecca and Scott Bell-Wesley, appeal to the Supreme Court of the State of Ames, from the final judgment entered in this action on the 13th day of May, 1983.

Dated: 21 May, 1983   Signed:_____
                                    Jane E. Harvey
                                    Attorney for Appellant (II)
                                    Llewellyn, Murray & Silber
                                    325 North Bridge Road
                                    Holmes, Ames

14

SUPERIOR COURT FOR THE STATE OF AMES

REBECCA AND SCOTT BELL-WESLEY,)
)
                Plaintiffs,   )   CIVIL ACTION 83-2004
)
        vs.   )
)   STIPULATION OF THE RECORD
DR. STEPHEN O'TOOLE,   )
)
                Defendant.   )

It is hereby stipulated by the attorneys for the respective parties in the above-named action, that the following shall constitute the transcript of the record on appeal.

1. Pleadings before the Superior Court of the State of Ames:

   a. Summons (omitted)

   b. Complaint

   c. Return of Service (omitted)

   d. Answer

   e. Affidavit of Service (omitted)

2. Findings of Fact & Conclusions of Law

3. Opinion of the Superior Court of the State of Ames

4. Judgment of the Superior Court of the State of Ames

5. Notice of Appeal

6. Trial Record

7. Exhibit A

8. This Designation

15

INSTRUCTIONS TO PARTICIPANTS

Assume that no arguable issue exists concerning:

1. Plaintiffs' timeliness in bringing the action under the relevant statute of limitations.

2. Defendant's negligence in performing the operation and in performing the sperm count upon which he relied in informing plaintiff Scott Bell-Wesley he was sterile.

3. The actual <u>amount</u> of damages as a goal upon appeal. Quantification and award of each element is determined upon remand; the issue then is whether the court should recognize each type of damage as recoverable.

Chapter III

RESEARCHING THE BRIEF

A. SOURCES AVAILABLE IN THE LIBRARY

Once you can recite the record in your sleep and you have given some consideration to a core theory, you are ready to begin the search for support for your affirmative arguments and ways to rebut the likely strong points of your adversary. Support is simply someone else (a "source") saying what you want to say. The stronger the authority, the better, but relevance without strength is better than strength without relevance.

Sources can be divided into three very general categories:

(1) Primary sources (the law itself);

(2) Secondary sources (commentaries about the law);

(3) Bridge sources (partly compilations of the law as it is generally understood, and partly discussion of that law).

1. Primary Sources. Primary sources are actual law in their jurisdiction. In the American system, there are numerous primary sources, including the United States Constitution and state constitutions. Congress and state legislatures create primary *statutory law.* Federal and state courts, by issuing opinions, create *common law.* (Note that court opinions are often interpretations of law derived from the other sources.) Federal and state agencies pass rules and regulations that fall into the category of *administrative law.* Primary sources are by far the strongest and most important sources for your argument. Most day-to-day legal research is done in this area.

Sometimes two primary sources can disagree on the state of the law. Suppose, for example, you discover that a state court opinion contradicts a federal statute. Which one do you follow? Binding authorities are those that must be followed by all lower courts and administrative bodies within that jurisdiction. Persuasive authorities are those that may carry a great deal of weight because of the body or person that created them, but need not be followed.

2. General Source Tools. Many moot court cases require you to write and speak intelligently on legal topics in which you have no expertise. This problem is not unique to moot court; when you leave law school, there will still be areas of the law about which you know nothing. When you need to learn about a legal area quickly, general sources can provide you with important background information.

Bridge sources and secondary sources can serve a general informative function. Bridge sources, like the Restatements of the Law and legal encyclopedias, contain summaries of the law from a broad perspective. They are useful in developing a working knowledge of the topic. Secondary sources, like law review articles and hornbooks, are generally written from a single perspective and often advance and support arguments on what the state of the law in an area should be. Both bridge and secondary sources may be cited in legal arguments.

a. Secondary sources. Secondary sources comment on primary sources. Included here are law review articles, treatises and hornbooks written by legal experts, and articles from publications and magazines that serve the legal profession. Secondary sources are often cited in legal arguments and opinions. They are most useful not as restatements of the law itself, but for discussions of how a legal principle is applied or interpreted, or where the law in a particular area has changed. The strength of secondary sources varies greatly, and usually is a direct function of the status of the particular author or publication.

In addition to providing helpful background information, a chapter in a hornbook or a journal article on point is particularly good for summarizing arguments made in support of or against cases that you may find relevant. Treatises, hornbooks, and articles generally direct you to important cases on the topic, which can save an enormous amount of time in the research process. Secondary sources are especially good at highlighting trends in the law. Although you cannot expect to find all of the required answers to a given legal problem in secondary sources, they are very helpful starting points.

b. Bridge sources. Bridge sources are partly compilations of primary sources and partly discussions of these sources. These generally have several authors and attempt to give an unbiased presentation of the law.

One common bridge source is the set of Restatements of the Law. The Restatements are the result of an effort by the American Law Institute to compile the common law into a set of convenient volumes. The laws of Agency, Contracts, Torts, Property, Trusts, Judgments, and Conflicts of Law have been "restated." Generally, the Restatements do not carry as much weight as primary sources; however, many state legislatures and courts have given parts of the Restatements primary source status over the years, and the Restatements are often cited in legal arguments and opinions as essentially binding statements of the law.

The Restatements, of course, are useful only insofar as they cover a particular subject. Legal encyclopedias, while not as persuasively authoritative, cover the entire range of legal subjects. The two most common encyclopedias are *Corpus Juris Secundum* ("C.J.S."), and *American Jurisprudence* ("Am.Jur."). They are often cited in legal arguments and opinions as important sources of information, serving the same function that a non-legal encyclopedia, such as the *Encyclopedia Brittanica,* would serve.

In addition to C.J.S. and Am.Jur., some states have their own legal encyclopedias. Notable examples are *New York Jurisprudence* and *Texas Jurisprudence.* State legal encyclopedias are often cited in state law cases and, depending on the state and the court, may carry a great deal of weight.

Legal encyclopedias are helpful in several respects. For example, you can find a general discussion of virtually any legal subject in *Corpus Juris Secundum.* C.J.S. is case annotated, so you will find citations to cases that deal with your subject. Finally, C.J.S. is published by West Publishing Company, and is tied into the West key number system, which is discussed in detail in Part B.2.a.(1) of this chapter. Under this system, West classifies legal subjects by topic name and number. You can use this topic name/key number combination to find cases, statutes, regulations, and other legal sources which are relevant to your subject.

American Jurisprudence can be used in this manner, but with a different system. Am.Jur. allows you access to the Lawyer's Cooperative system, described in Part B.2.a.(2). Within Am.Jur., you will find a discussion of the general area of law in which you are interested. You will also find citations to relevant cases. Further, you may find references to *American Law Reports* ("A.L.R."), which is a compilation of both cases and legal articles. More will be said about A.L.R. later in this section.

State legal encyclopedias work in the same way, and contain references to cases and articles which deal with the law of that state.

When using legal encyclopedias, as well as many other legal references, be certain to check the "pocket part" on the inside back cover of each volume. The pocket part is a supplement to the original volume, and is sent out periodically by the publisher. It contains references to changes or updates in the law that have occurred since the original volume went to press. It is important to check the pocket part for two reasons: (1) to make certain that the law on which you are relying is still valid, and (2) to find recently published sources relevant to your issue.

B. THE MECHANICS OF LEGAL RESEARCH

The authorities described above are useful to you only if you can find the various cases, articles, and treatises that deal with your particular issues. This section explains how to find relevant material by using the tools available for legal research.

Before beginning, however, a word of caution is in order. Seldom will one issue lead you to one publication and one answer. Indeed, normally you will discover bits of an answer here and pieces of an answer there. Thus, it is useful to think of the various publications as part of a large, interconnected system. There are many paths from many points to many answers, and you can usually get from any place within the system to any other place, so long as you use the tools properly. Keep this in mind as you read the materials that follow.

1. General Sources. Research in secondary and bridge sources is most like the research done in areas outside the law. Secondary source books are catalogued like any other volume and kept on the library shelves. Magazines and law reviews are indexed in publications much like the *Readers' Guide To Periodical Literature*, which you probably used when doing non-specialized research in college.

Whether multi-volume or a single book, hornbooks and treatises are always indexed. You must turn to the index to locate the portion of the book dealing with your issue. Different sources are indexed differently, and you must acquaint yourself with each system and learn how to use it effectively.

Law reviews and magazine articles on legal subjects are easily located through two publications: *Index to Legal Periodicals* and *Current Law Index*. Both publications list articles according to author and subject. They are published monthly. Be aware that the indexes are not cumulative. Thus, you must gather the indexes for the time span in which you are interested and look in each for appropriate articles. There is also a microform index, *Legal Resources Index*, which is cumulative and lists law-related articles from 1980 to the present.

2. Primary Sources. Most legal research is directed to primary sources: the law itself. The reason for this is obvious; you will not be able to determine where your case stands with respect to the law until you know exactly what that law is. Thus, you should never lose sight of the fact that, in most cases, your ultimate goal is to find primary sources. The research tools described in this section are designed to help you reach that goal.

Be aware that the order in which the various tools are discussed is of no particular significance. For most legal questions, they can be used in any order you choose. For very narrow questions, of course, you may direct your research to a specific source. For example, if you merely wish to find the elements of criminal fraud in a particular jurisdiction, you may go directly to that jurisdiction's criminal code. If, however, you wish to determine how those elements have been interpreted by the courts in that jurisdiction, you will have to extend your search to court opinions. This section discusses the use of the following research tools: (a) case reporter/ digest systems; (b) statutes; (c) regulations; (d) case annotated research tools; and (e) the *Shepard's Citations* system.

a. Case Reporter/Digest Systems

(1) *The West System.* Reporters and digests are collections of court opinions and case summaries, respectively. Because the West system is the most extensive, it is described first. There are five simple steps to follow in using the West reporter system:

(a) Make a *subject/jurisdiction determination;*

(b) Look up the subject(s) in the proper *Descriptive Word Index;*

(c) Follow the reference in the Descriptive Word Index to the *case digest;*

(d) Read the *case summaries* in the case digest to determine whether any cases are relevant, and then record the citations of all relevant cases; and

(e) Use the citations to find the fully printed cases in the *reporters.*

(a) *Subject/jurisdiction determination.* You must begin by determining the legal subject(s) you wish to research, and the jurisdiction(s) in which you wish to focus that research. For example, in *Bell-Wesley v. O'Toole,* you would be most interested in state law, because the wrongful birth tort is covered by state law. Those cases heard in federal court because of diversity jurisdiction will be included in digests covering the state law that the federal court was interpreting. However, the case itself would appear in a federal reporter. Because Ames is a mythical jurisdiction, counsel in *Bell-Wesley v. O'Toole* would be interested in the laws of many states. If, however, the case was in a Texas court, counsel could go directly to the Texas Digest or the Southwest Reporter Digest. Because West's General Digest covers all state and federal law, it would be a good place to start researching when your moot court case is set in a mythical jurisdiction. It is rather cumbersome to use, however, so you may want to go to the several regional reporters. These include only the law in the states covered by the reporter. Substantively, you would be looking under areas such as Torts, Wrongful Birth, and Damages.

(b) *Descriptive Word Index.* The Descriptive Word Index is an alphabetical listing of topics located at the end of each set of case digest volumes. (Under the West system, there is a set of case digests and a descriptive word index for every reporter except the Northeastern Reporter.) Look up the subject in the proper index. In *Bell-Wesley v. O'Toole,* you can use the index for the General Digest. Under the general heading, "Torts," you find the subheading, "Damages." If you wish to look for even more specific topics, look at the entries below "Mitigation or Set-off." For our example, look under "Wrongful Birth." Next to that entry you will find, in slightly darker print, the entry, "Phys 18.110." This entry is the *topic name* ("Phys," which stands for "Physicians & Surgeons") and *key number* (18.110) for your subject. Record this information.

(c) *Case digests.* Now turn to the case digests themselves. Topics in the digests are also listed in alphabetical (according to topic name) and numerical (according to key number) order. Look up the topic name and key number in the case digests. In this example, you should turn to the volume containing the topic "Physicians & Surgeons" and find the entries for key number 18.110.

(d) *Case summaries.* Under "Physicians & Surgeons 18.110" in the digest there is a collection of cases relevant to your inquiry. Record the case citations of any cases which seem of particular interest. You should also check the pocket part to see whether any pertinent cases have been decided more recently. In this example you would probably notice the case summary for *Hartke v. McKelway*, 707 F.2d 1544 (D.C.Cir.1983), which states that parents who have a healthy child cannot be said to be damaged in a wrongful birth claim. This case appears to discuss directly one of the issues determined at the very beginning of the research process.

(e) *Reporters.* Finally, use the citations to find the fully printed cases in the reporters. In our example, you would find *Hartke v. McKelway* in the Federal Reporter, Second Series ("F.2d"), volume 707 at page 1544.

Many students wonder why it is necessary to read the entire case after having already read the case summary in the digest. Simply put, the case summaries are prepared by the West staff, and not by the court issuing the opinion. Consequently, although they are usually accurate, they cannot be considered statements of the law. The fully printed case, however, is a primary source of law.

(2) *The Lawyer's Cooperative System.* In addition to the West reporting system, Lawyer's Cooperative has a modified reporting system, *American Law Reports* ("A.L.R."), which is a cross between a reporter and a legal encyclopedia. A.L.R. contains a limited number of "significant" cases. Consequently, it is not as useful or thorough a reporting system as the West system. However, A.L.R. also includes articles about the topics covered in the reported cases. Thus, if you find an A.L.R. article on your particular subject, you will have a quick review of the case law in that area.

There are two basic steps to follow in using the Lawyer's Cooperative system:

(a) Look up your subject in the A.L.R. Quick Index; and

(b) Follow the reference to the volumes of the *American Law Reports* where you will find both fully printed cases and articles.

As mentioned above, *American Jurisprudence* is a part of the Lawyer's Cooperative system. You will find references to Am.Jur. in A.L.R. and vice versa.

b. Statutes. In order to find statutes, go to the statutory code of the jurisdiction in which you are interested, and look up your subject in the code index. If your subject is governed by statutory law, there will be a reference to a particular statute. You then simply look up the statute in the code. Remember to check the pocket part in both the index and the code—legislatures often pass laws on new subjects and often change or repeal old laws.

c. Regulations. Finding regulations is similar to finding statutes. Simply use the regulation code index in the applicable jurisdiction to find your subject. Then follow the reference to the proper regulation within the code. Again, check the pocket parts.

d. Case annotated research tools. Case annotated tools are those research tools that contain references to case law. Common case annotated tools are legal encyclopedias, such as C.J.S. and Am. Jur., where references to illustrative cases are included in the discussions of the various legal subjects. As previously mentioned, law review articles, hornbooks, and treatises will also provide helpful, relevant case cites.

Statutory codes are often case annotated. For example, West publishes the *United States Code* in an annotated version, *United States Code Annotated* ("U.S.C.A."), which refers to cases interpreting the particular statute. Most state codes also contain references to pertinent cases. By using annotated codes, you can find not only particular statutes, but court opinions which interpreted those statutes. Note also that U.S.C.A. and many of the state statutory codes are published by West, and therefore are tied into the West key number system.

A court opinion itself may be thought of as an annotated source. For example, judges in their opinions cite numerous cases, statutes, regulations, legal encyclopedias, and other sources of law. By reading just one case, you are directed to many other possibly useful sources.

The West system provides another example of the case as an annotated source. In West reporters, court opinions are preceded by headnotes which are summaries of the points of law dealt with in the opinion itself. Headnotes are useful in two ways. First, a quick look at the headnotes can tell you whether or not this particular opinion addresses the issues in which you are interested. Second, each headnote is given a topic name and key number, and is thus tied in to the rest of the West system. The headnotes from one case can lead you to many other sources. Thus, you may be able to begin research without consulting an index or an encyclopedia—all you need is a single case!

e. Shepard's Citation System. The Shepard's Citation system ("Shepard's") can best be understood by analogy. Suppose that a playwright produces his own play. Night after night, month after month (and year after year, if the play is successful), the play goes on in theaters across the country. Over the years the playwright keeps a scrapbook of the reviews that the play has received. From time to time he updates a list he started on opening night—a list with abbreviated entries that mention the city in which the play was staged, the name of any publications that printed reviews, and whether or not the reviews were favorable. By using the list alone, the playwright can tell, in a general sense, how well the play has fared in different cities at different times. If he wishes to find out exactly what any particular reviewer has said, he may refer to the scrapbook.

Shepard's is to sources of the law what the list is to the scrapbook of reviews. It is a history, in abbreviated form, of the subsequent treatment of legal sources. Like the list kept by the playwright, Shepard's tells you nothing about the substance of the source. Rather, it tells you where and how you can find the source, and, to some extent, whether or not its "reviews" were favorable.

As a legal researcher, you will be interested in knowing how subsequent "reviewers" have treated a particular source. You will want to know whether the source you wish to use is still good law, or whether it has been changed, replaced, or overruled. You will also want to locate any favorable "reviews" in order to use them to support your position. Shepard's is the device which allows you to do this.

In order to use Shepard's you must begin with a cited legal authority. Assume that during your research you discovered a New York opinion which supported your argument. You want to determine whether it is still valid law. At the same time you would like to find other cases which have cited the opinion, and which presumably would support your position. The citation for your original case is 301 N.Y.S.2d 519. You should follow these four steps.

(1) *Locate the proper set of Shepard's citators.* Shepard's has citators corresponding to each of the reporter systems in which a case may be cited, i.e. official reporters, unofficial reporters, specialty reporters, etc. Shepard's also has citators chronicling treatment of the United States Constitution, federal statutes, federal regulations, and the Restatements of Law. For this example, you should find a set of citators that covers the New York Supplement (Second Series),

beginning with the first citator in which volume 301 appeared. Note that for all but the most recent cases, you will need to refer to the citator in which your authority first appeared, plus all subsequent supplementary citators in which the authority will continue to appear. (Shepard's is updated every month and compiled every several years.) It is vitally important to remember that the volumes are not cumulative. You must look in each volume of the citator in which you are working if it could contain a cite to the case that you are shepardizing.

(2) *Look up the cite in the citator.* For this example, you should look up volume 301, page 519 in the citator.

(3) *Check to see how subsequent "reviewers" have treated the case.* This is done by referring to the small letters to the left of the list of citations. These letters are the abbreviations Shepard's uses to indicate how the original case has been treated. A list of Shepard's abbreviations and their meanings is found at the front of every Shepard's citator. For example, "o" means the cited case overruled the original case, "c" means the original case was criticized, and "j" means a judge cited the original case in a dissenting opinion. In this example, you will note that different authorities have treated the original case quite differently. In order to determine whether or not the original case is still valid law, you will want to check the cases that criticized it and perhaps some of the later cases that cited it, but for which there is no notation. (No notation simply means that the case was cited as authority for one of its principles of law.) At the end of the list of citations you will find a number of citations to law review articles and A.L.R. annotations that have mentioned the case.

(4) *Use the notations to find supporting authority.* In order to find support for the position taken by the original case, look to the cases which either followed it (signified by "f"), or to cases which cited it, but for which there is no notation.

Note that the first three steps are used to validate the original case, while the final step is used to direct the researcher to other relevant sources. One final word about Shepard's: so long as you are only checking the continuing validity of the case, you may stop at step three. But if you intend to use Shepard's for research, be aware that the letter notations are extremely narrow with respect to what they can convey. Even the notation "o" only means that the case itself was overruled. It does not tell you why it was overruled or on which point of law. Thus it would be advisable to read that case before giving up on your original case.

To increase the precision of your Shepard's research even further, you can use the West headnotes, and restrict your search to cites which have mentioned only the portion of the case which interests you. For example, if the first headnote in the case that you are shepardizing dealt with applying the benefits rule to a wrongful birth case, and that was the only part of the case that interested you, you could look in the citator for all cites to that case which have a tiny exponent "1" listed after the reporter. That means that the court (or other source) in the cite listed specifically cited the case for *that* issue, i.e., the issue raised in headnote "1," the benefits rule issue. This technique can save needless hours of chasing down cites that are not relevant to the issue that you are researching.

C. DATA BASES AND COMPUTERIZED RESEARCH

Computerized legal research has developed considerably since its introduction in the early 1970s. Many lawyers today rely on the speed and accuracy of computerized data bases in both the exploratory and final stages of their research. Because a computer can search rapidly through its vast storage capacity in response to a search command, computer-aided research can quickly and effectively augment traditional research methods. For example, it is easy to request opinions written by a particular judge or in a particular circuit on a specific topic. Since data bases are kept very current, computer searches are especially helpful for updating and for investigating newly emerging areas of the law. Despite the prevalence of Westlaw and Lexis in law libraries and offices, students still need to learn traditional research methods because they provide a different means of approaching legal issues which can augment computer searches. Traditional research is also more cost effective for certain types of research.

Westlaw is available through West Publishing Company and offers full texts of opinions plus the synopses, headnotes, and key numbers of West reporters. Lexis, a product of Mead Data Central, is a comprehensive full text system which includes federal and state cases. Both Lexis and Westlaw contain special libraries (like federal tax or securities cases) and Shepard's Citations. Auto-Cite, developed by Lawyer's Cooperative Publishing Company and available on Lexis, provides appellate histories of cases. Insta-Cite, a product of West Publishing Company, provides similar information to Westlaw users.

Each system has its own training program, available through libraries, subscribers, or the company itself, and those programs are the only way to learn the best research strategies.

D. TIPS FOR RESEARCHING

Always leave good footprints. Make careful notes of where you have been. Make sure to write down parallel cites, numbers of pages from which you have extracted quotations, and other data that are infinitely easier to scrawl down while the source is in front of you than while the typewriter is humming with your final brief in it.

Never, absolutely never, cite a case without reading it. Read all of it. Headnotes cannot capture critical nuances. Be sensitive to how each case could be distinguished and differentiated on the basis of its facts.

Take good notes while you are reading the case. Even the most trustworthy memory won't be able to keep the facts of the twenty-second case straight.

Be thorough! The West system is not perfect in pigeonholing cases exactly where you might think they should be filed in the key number system. One safety precaution is to read cases cited in other relevant cases until you start finding the same cases again and again. Also, check the key numbers following and preceding yours to make sure West is not subdividing your topic.

Recognize the importance of being recent. Everyone has his own horror story of missing that recent case. Always check the pocket part and familiarize yourself with other techniques for finding the most recent declarations for each variety of tribunal, and the rules of your forum court governing the use of brand-new or unreported authority. If the authority post-dates the brief, there are generally some notice requirements that need to be followed.

E. CONCLUSION

These are the common tools of legal research. It should be stressed again that by treating the various tools as part of an overall system of legal information, you can create a research strategy that will lead you to your ultimate goal: the primary sources of the law relevant to the issue you are researching. Although much of this will seem complicated at first, rest assured that by following the steps outlined above for each tool you will become an effective and efficient legal researcher.

One final note about research tools; there exist many other research systems for certain specialized areas of the law. For example, those of you who will practice federal communications law will discover the Pike and Fisher system which collects the rules, regulations, and opinions of the Federal Communications Commission. Commercial lawyers will find helpful the Uniform Commercial Code Reporting Service. Indeed, there are specialized reporters and research aids for many areas of the law, including aviation, admiralty, tax, securities, and labor. By checking the card catalogue in your law library, you will be able to determine what types of materials are on hand. Generally speaking, these tools are used in the same way as the more common tools: you begin with an issue and follow various references until you reach the relevant primary sources of law.

Chapter IV

WRITING THE BRIEF

A. INTRODUCTION

1. **The Purpose of the Brief.** A brief systematically presents the arguments, authorities and relevant background material of a legal controversy and aids an appellate court in rendering a decision. Because of the large number of cases heard by each court, judges today must rely on briefs as the foundation of their decision-making process. A brief gives each party an equal opportunity to describe her position clearly, accurately, and assertively to the appellate court.

As an instrument of persuasion, the brief must be simple and interesting, with a compelling factual and legal foundation. Because the brief often serves as the court's resource for writing the opinion, the document must be complete and reliable. Strong advocacy requires the briefwriter to craft a fair and persuasive piece of writing that will lead the court to the writer's point of view rather than bombard it with conclusory statements.

2. **Comparing Briefwriting and Oral Advocacy.** Effective advocacy requires that the brief and the oral argument be planned together. Each has strengths and weaknesses as a tool of persuasion and as a means of conveying information. Numbers and dates are better absorbed visually than aurally and should therefore be emphasized in the brief. Also, the brief is the appropriate place to cite authority; citations flow more smoothly off the pen than off the tongue. Only through oral argument, however, can you sense the reactions of your audience and adjust your presentation to meet their concerns. Your brief should contain all of the information necessary for the court to reach a decision, while the oral argument gives you a chance to have a conversation with the court and to rebut arguments that your opponent raised in her brief that you did not deal with in yours. Devise your appellate game plan by recognizing the strategic values of the brief and the oral argument and exploiting the strengths of each.

3. **Stylistic Guidelines.** The writing skills you learned elsewhere apply equally well to legal writing. Those who enjoy writing in general may be surprised to learn that they enjoy writing briefs. The same challenges of imagination, phrasing, and structure must be met to yield a successful product. It has been said that there is no such thing as "legal" writing, and there is undoubtedly much truth to that statement. The general principles of prose writing that helped you turn out cogent collegiate papers should not be abandoned at the

law school's door. (And, of course, it is never too late to learn or relearn those principles.) Always keep in mind, however, that a brief is a persuasive piece of writing and each element of it should be geared toward convincing the court of the correctness of your position.

Recall the basic guidelines for writing your brief: it should be simple, interesting, complete, and reliable. Within those constraints, you have considerable discretion in selecting what writing style to use. Opinions differ as to what tone is ultimately the most persuasive. Many advocates adhere to a dispassionate, scholarly approach, relying heavily on authorities. Others prefer an aggressively adversarial tack, constantly going for "the jugular," building drama and emotion, and decimating the assertions of the other side. Still others combine elements of both extremes.

Whatever tone you decide to use, general considerations of style still apply. Archibald Cox has repeatedly observed that a brief should march, and a good brief should sing while it marches. Some basic marching orders follow.

Strategically select every word by analyzing its tactical and literary value. Be careful, for example, when choosing the names for the parties in your case. The overuse of "appellant" and "appellee" in a brief can be confusing to a reader who does not share your intimate understanding of the record. Instead, characterize the parties in a manner that will influence the reader's perception of them. A brief adopting a formalistic approach should be formal in naming the parties (e.g., "Parent," "Doctor"). A brief appealing to the court's sense of equity would probably use more personal titles (e.g., "the Bell-Wesleys," "Dr. O'Toole"). Another device is to try to evoke the reader's empathy for your client by referring to him with a personal title and using a more formal title for his adversary.

Realize the potential of various parts of speech for conveying emphasis. A forceful argument will contain action verbs, rather than only forms of the verb "to be." "Spot bit Jane" describes the scenario more dramatically than does the passive construction "Jane was bitten by Spot." However, when presenting damaging facts and arguments you can subtly downplay their force by using the passive voice.

Do not rely on complex, pompous language. Legalese is not inherently persuasive and should not be used except in exceptional circumstances. Simplify your language. Your eloquence will not suffer and you will enhance the force of your arguments. Long sentences, multisyllabic words, and multiple subordinate clauses are generally out of place in a brief.

Avoid using extended quotations. A paraphrase with a citation better demonstrates how a case that you have researched aids your position, and an impatient reader is likely to skip over a lengthy quotation. Explain the relevance of the case yourself. Don't use a long quotation and expect the court to figure out how the case applies.

B. THE PARTS OF THE BRIEF

A brief consists of various parts, each designed to convey a specific type of information. The parts are: (1) the questions presented; (2) the facts; (3) the arguments supporting the writer's position; and (4) a conclusion. Each component has a separate but complementary purpose so that the whole can function as a persuasive instrument.

1. Questions Presented. First, the brief must set the agenda for the court by presenting what questions must be answered in order to decide the case. As Judge Tate of the Fourth Circuit once noted, "A judge's initial reaction to the seriousness and merit of the appeal is often based upon this indication of what the counsel considers to be vital to his case."[1] Like the brief as a whole, the questions themselves must be simple, interesting, complete, and reliable.

Crafting the questions presented is a useful exercise with which to begin writing your brief because it forces you to put your thoughts into complete, sensible sentences. Some people, however, prefer to save this task for last, after they have articulated their argument in detail. Either way, plan to spend a lot of time writing and rewriting the questions. They create the first impression of your version of the issues for the judge. Don't waste this initial opportunity for advocacy.

a. How many? You should give some thought to the number of questions presented as you create your core theory. In making this decision, determine how many winning arguments are on your side. Avoid weakening your strong points by associating them with less momentous arguments. These considerations, in conjunction with space restrictions, will probably leave you with two, three, or to really push it, four arguments in your brief.

b. Structure. Usually placed at the beginning of the text, the questions presented are a structural requirement of every brief. Present them in the order in which their corresponding arguments will appear in the brief. Each question should be self-sufficient, requiring no reference to any point contained in a previous one. (For

---

[1] Tate, The Art of Brief-Writing: What a Judge Wants to Read, 4 Litig. 11 (Winter 1978).

example, do not say, "Is *such action* prohibited by the Establishment Clause?")

The questions should incorporate the facts of your case and the law you wish applied to it. This enables you to impart some of the flavor of your argument to the reader from the moment he picks up the brief. Fact-filled questions are almost always more interesting (and hence more powerful) than formless, abstract questions of law. However, some advocates believe that a question studded with facts and laden with dependent clauses is far too complex, and that a simpler, abstract question actually has more power. At the very least, the questions presented must serve as signposts for your arguments and indicate which side you are arguing. They should plant the first seeds of persuasion, even when they serve as labels rather than fact-filled lead-ins. Experiment with different types of questions presented, but keep in mind that it is probably better to err on the side of including facts than on that of ignoring them.

c. Examples. Different advocates arguing *Bell-Wesley v. O'Toole* might draft the following questions presented:

Abstract:

Is a doctor who negligently performs a vasectomy liable to a couple which subsequently has a child for the costs of raising that child?

Fact-Filled:

If a "wrongful birth" claim is created, should the damages claimed by the parents be offset by the extensive benefits they derive from their healthy child or reduced due to the parents' failure to mitigate damages through the reasonable measures of having amniocentesis performed or placing the "unwanted" child up for adoption?

Make sure that your questions suggest the answer that you want the court to reach. You want to suggest that given this particular problem, the court can only reasonably rule one way. However, be careful not to inspire irritation at your overly biased presentation or suggest by your stridency the inevitable counter-argument.

Consider these examples:

Not far enough:

Is a doctor who negligently performs a vasectomy liable for the costs of raising a child when the husband subsequently impregnates his wife and they have an unplanned baby?

Too far:

Where a couple, after having several congenitally deformed children who died soon after birth, has a child conceived after an unsuccessfully performed vasectomy, having refused to abort, give up for adoption, or otherwise get rid of the child, should the doctor who performed the vasectomy be held liable for all the costs of raising that child when in fact the couple could well afford to have the child, and in fact benefited from the doctor's negligence by receiving the healthy child that they had always wanted?

Just right:

Should a doctor whose repeated negligent performance of a sterilization inflicted numerous injuries upon an innocent couple be held responsible for the full extent of his negligence, including the medical costs, the physical and emotional pain and suffering, and the extensive financial costs associated with the birth of a child?

Questions presented should be answerable by either a yes or a no. There is a school of briefwriting that suggests that all of the appellant's questions should be answered by "yes" if the appellant's position prevails, while the status quo-loving appellee should consistently search for a negative response. There is a pleasing symmetry, if nothing else, to be gained from this approach. Some people try to frame all of the questions in a given brief so that they are answered the same way, either all "yes" or all "no," in support of your position.

2. The Introduction. Use of an introduction to the arguments in the brief has become more common in recent years. A one-paragraph road map of the essential facts and the course of the advocate's arguments is often quite useful to judges, particularly in complex cases. The introduction should be clear, concise, and devoid of citations. Rules governing the permissible location of an introduction vary by jurisdiction.

3. The Statement of Facts. The Statement of Facts, sometimes called the Statement of the Case, tells your view of what happened in the "real world" to throw this case into court. Both sides must present a complete and reliable, yet simple and interesting, version of the facts of the case. The facts are the material from which you draw your arguments. The way you relate the facts to the judge should make her ready to rule in your favor after reading them.

a. What are facts? Facts can be divided into two categories. There are substantive facts, concerned with events that happened before the litigation and at trial, and procedural facts, describing the legal path that the case has taken up to now. Some advocates present these two types of facts separately, others combine them in a general statement of the case. Both types of facts should be included, although such a formal division is not usually necessary for cases with short procedural histories.

You must also sort out the relevant facts from the irrelevant ones contained in the record. The decision as to what is relevant is often a commonsense one. Normally, any fact actually used to support either side's position will be relevant. All the relevant facts, in favor of and against your position, must be in the statement of the case.

b. Sticking to the record. You must, as a general rule, use only the facts presented in the "four corners" of the record. However, there are limited exceptions. You can draw inferences from facts in the record. You can use facts subject to "judicial notice." Use admissions of the other side as positive proof of a fact that you wish to establish. Use hypothetical facts and conjure up a "parade of horribles" which will eventually ensue if the argument that you present is not accepted.

The creativity that you demonstrate in presenting a persuasive fact situation must not, under any circumstances, extend to making up information. A judge will not let a fabricated fact slide by as a clever inference. An appellate court must rely on the record. All assumptions of fact must be firmly grounded in the record. Certain undeniable assertions, however, such as the fact that apples do not fall up, can be introduced without appearing in the record. Other information, like the conclusions of relevant sociological studies, can be used even though they are not part of the record as long as proper authority is cited. (For examples of citations to the record, see the Statements of Facts in both briefs in *Bell-Wesley v. O'Toole*.)

Remember when doing your research that you are researching the potential legal arguments that can be used to support your position. You cannot, as an appellate attorney, research new evidence, or make it up.

However, holes in the record are not necessarily useless. You can successfully use "negative facts" to buttress your position. Negative facts are facts that the other side can neither establish nor disprove because of holes in the record. The advocate can effectively use negative facts to create a gap of essential knowledge, requiring a ruling in her client's favor. For example, a defendant-appellee may show that the plaintiff-appellant never met his burden of proof by pointing to the absence in the record of facts indicating otherwise. Or the advocate can fill a hole with hypotheticals, each as likely as the next, all designed to demonstrate the invalidity of her opponent's position given this lack of vital information. For example, the *Bell-Wesley v. O'Toole* record is silent on the issue of whether Scott and Rebecca considered placing Frank for adoption. Nonetheless, in the appellants' statement of the case, one sentence reads: "[a]lthough they could have adopted a child, they instead chose to devote their time and energy to their careers and each other." (See p. 58.) Do not be afraid to make effective use of holes in the record: holes have won many cases for clever appellate attorneys.

   c. Organizing facts. The organization of the facts also serves to further the goals of the brief. Every word in the statement of facts should be geared toward making the brief a better instrument of persuasion or a more complete and reliable resource.

   A chronological narrative may or may not be the most persuasive structure for telling your story. "This happened, then that happened" probably lends an air of routineness to the activities depicted, which may or may not be the image you wish to convey. Consider starting with the conflict or the injury, if appropriate. Never forget to consider the impact of the specific words that you choose. Use active verbs for your strong points. Use labels that will appropriately characterize the parties. Attempt to use the connotations of words effectively. Make sure, also, to take it from square one. Introduce the characters and spell out abbreviations. Don't let your statement of the facts leave the court with needless questions.

   d. Adverse facts. Reliability is essential. You cannot have any glaring omissions of adverse facts in your statement, because they will certainly be central to the other side's case. This kind of unreliability decreases your credibility with the court. The negative side of the case will appear less damaging if you cautiously disclose it first.

   There are ways of downplaying the dangerous, of course. Passive verbs can dilute the force of statements. The offending material can be placed in a subordinate clause. Also, once you have hung out your dirty laundry there is no need to wave it. For example, while an appellant needs to disclose that there was an adverse judgment below, she need not disclose that the district judge rejected each and every contention. Rest assured that the appellee will mention that. For example, in the *Bell-Wesley v. O'Toole* briefs, the doctor's attorney referred to his client's negligence by saying Dr. O'Toole "misperformed" the sterilization. On the other hand, the Bell-Wesleys' attorney characterized the same act as "repeated negligence" in performing both the vasectomy and the sperm count.

   e. Fact versus argument. Your desire to paint a persuasive factual picture must not cross the boundary into argument. You risk invoking the court's ire and losing credibility if you markedly slant the facts. In the end, facts must remain facts. They are used to support your conclusions; they must not be used as conclusions. For example, you can emphasize the defendant's obviously improvident actions, but you should not label them as negligent unless you also remind the court that the plaintiff charged the defendant with negligence. In making arguments substantiated by holes in the record, for example, mention the holes in your Statement of the

Facts, but explain the significance of the lack of information in the argument section of the brief. It is up to the court to draw the legal conclusion once you have persuasively pointed it out.

4. The Arguments. The arguments comprise the body of the brief. By this point, you have selected the few arguments that you will present. You have tossed out weaker or less clear ones because including them might dilute the force of your main points. You have buttressed your ideas with the necessary authority. You have anticipated, preempted, or rebutted your opponent's crucial arguments and have distinguished his key cases. Now the only thing left to do is write.

a. Argument headings. Each argument begins with an argument heading, in capital letters, single spaced. These set out the argument made in that subsection of the brief. The headings should be complete sentences.

Your questions presented will provide the foundation for the argument headings, which state affirmatively the resolution of the issues framed in the questions. They should be responsive to your question presented for that particular issue. An aggressive argument heading will clue the reader in to the applicable law, to the way in which the law applies to the facts of the case, and to the conclusion that follows from that application. If this proves too difficult, an argument heading, like a question presented, may instead be a simple signpost or title for the argument.

b. Subheadings. Subheadings can be used to summarize and partition lengthy arguments. They are typed in lower case, with initial capitals, and are underscored. When an argument is relatively simple, as in many moot court briefs, subheadings should be avoided so that the general flow of the argument is uninterrupted. (For examples of argument headings and subheadings, see both briefs for *Bell-Wesley v. O'Toole*.)

c. Organization and structure of arguments. In organizing your brief, phrase your arguments in the affirmative and put the strongest ones first.

The introductory paragraph of your argument should be just that—an introduction to what is to follow. It is like a topic sentence for the entire argument. A good general format for any argument is the pattern of a logical syllogism. Your argument would then look something like this:

—Introductory statement of the legal standard, framed in terms of this case;

—Application of the facts of the case to that legal standard;

—Conclusion;

—Rebuttal of opponent's assertion on this point.

The first sentence of each paragraph must be a topic sentence that tells the reader what will be discussed in that paragraph. A good test of the logical structure and cohesiveness of your brief is to read the first sentence of each paragraph. If this scan gives you a complete idea of the facts of your case and of the legal reasoning that you are using, then you are on the right track. If it doesn't, then it is time to reorganize and rewrite.

d. Rebuttal and preemption of arguments. Careful drafting of the rebuttal to your opponent's arguments will help reinforce your core theory and keep the judge from agreeing too readily with your adversary. Never make conclusory statements characterizing your opponent's position as dead wrong, because she will probably have mounted a relatively convincing case and your blanket dismissal will only detract from your own credibility. Instead, try to show the illogic of the argument, to demonstrate how the facts fail to support the legal conclusion, and to point out the unfortunate consequences that would flow from a decision for your opponent. Criticize the authority used as unpersuasive or off point. But remember, attack the argument, not your opponent.

Most moot court programs use a staggered exchange system that resembles that of most appellate courts. The appellant files her brief first, then the appellee files his brief in response. Occasionally the appellant has the option of filing a second, shorter brief in reply to the appellee.

The appellee, because of his position as respondent, will spend more time rebutting and will have the advantage of knowing exactly what to rebut because he will have seen his opponent's brief. Appellant does not have this opportunity to highlight weaknesses in her adversary's brief unless she does so in the reply brief, or in oral argument. Plan accordingly.

Of course, due to the limited time between the filing of the appellant's brief and the due date for the appellee's response, the appellee must do most of his research and outline his arguments before he receives his opponent's brief. When it comes to writing, a point-by-point refutation is often not the ideal format for an appellee's brief. Arguments independent of those raised by the appellant are often stronger and more persuasive.

Neither side should give an argument that it is rebutting too much importance by spending a lot of time on it, or by putting it first in the brief. The tone of each brief must remain affirmative and not convey a totally defensive posture. Remember that oral argument is sometimes a better time to confront your opponent's arguments. In the brief, just recognize that there is another view and deal with it quickly.

5. The Conclusion. The brief should end with a section entitled "Conclusion," in which you state the result you seek to achieve. Some people stop there. Others go on to summarize their arguments and delineate the relief they want the court to grant. If you use this more expansive approach, you may have to incorporate the applicable scope of review. Make sure that you have actually argued everything that appears in the conclusion, and that your summary restates your position in recognizable form. If you do anything more than state the desired result, you may choose to work your core theory into the conclusion.

C.   USE OF AUTHORITY

Authorities are not glorified punctuation marks that must appear at the conclusion of every sentence in a brief. Rather, when properly used, they aid in convincing the reader of the correctness of the propositions asserted. The fact that someone other than you has thought about and given support for a certain idea will make most judges more likely to support it themselves. It's not that the judges won't trust you, but you are recognized as having a certain bias, and sound use of authorities enhances your persuasiveness.

When selecting authorities to use in a citation, choose the ones with the greatest relevance (generally referred to as being "on point") and the greatest weight, based on their sources. Since many moot court cases are set in mythical jurisdictions and are cases of first impression, opinions from the Supreme Court of the United States, a well-regarded federal circuit court, or a state court of last resort are the most persuasive sources. You may also cite a variety of jurisdictions to indicate that a given proposition is spreading like wildfire through the judiciary. In this situation, of course, three cases from three states will be more effective than three cases from one state.

1.   Use of Parentheticals. Uncontested propositions of law, such as the definition of negligence, rarely require more than one authority in a citation. Nothing is to be gained from merely stringing citations together. Put in the authority that you need to achieve credibility and stop there.

In many instances the most effective way to use a case is to paraphrase the principle it stands for and follow that with a citation. However, judges are not familiar with most reported decisions, and they and their law clerks have neither the time nor the energy to read them all. Unless an authority supports only a general principle, an unelaborated or "bare" cite, giving only the case name and the reporter, will not help the court. Parentheticals, abstracting the facts of the case and/or quoting critical language, aid the reader by explaining the relevance, similarity, or difference of the cited case to the case at hand. Reading the footnotes in a hornbook will give you a feel for how to summarize cases in this way. (For examples of explanatory parentheticals, refer to the briefs in *Bell-Wesley v. O'Toole.*)

Cases that are particularly crucial to your argument, such as those propounding a rule that you seek to follow, may need more extensive treatment than a parenthetical. You may devote a small paragraph to explaining how the legal principle in that case governs the issue now before the court, or why it must be distinguished. Remember: in either situation, argue your own facts.

2. Signals. Signals, such as *"See," "E.g.," "Cf.,"* and *"But see"* are used to indicate how the cited authority bears on your case. The rules governing their use must be observed and mastered. See Chapter V, General Rules of Style and Citation of Authorities, for more specific examples, and consult *A Uniform System of Citation* (13th ed. 1981) for its latest promulgations.

For the sake of reliability and completeness, important cases standing *against* the propositions advanced in the brief should be cited. Signal them with *"But see"* or *"Contra"* and, if possible, distinguish them. They will undoubtedly be cited by the opposition, and you may be able to reduce their impact by undermining their logic, or distinguishing them on their facts. Citation of contrary authority lets the court know that you have been thorough, and may help negate any damage done by the adverse cases.

D. FORMALITIES

Now that you've done the hard work, you can preoccupy yourself with some technical details needed to make your brief look like a brief.

1. Title Page. A title page provides the relevant information about the case: the court, the docket number, the names of the parties, the names of the attorneys, and the date and place of hearing.

A full designation of the parties (e.g., "Plaintiff-Appellant") should appear on the title page, but need not be repeated anywhere else in the brief. In most state jurisdictions and lower federal courts, the original order of the parties is maintained in the case on appeal. The Supreme Court of the United States names the appealing party first.

Counsels' names, formal title (e.g., "Attorney for the Appellee"), and the date and place of the oral argument are placed in the lower right hand corner.

2. Table of Contents. The table of contents should list the components of the brief, including argument headings, subheadings, and the conclusion, along with the page number on which they can be found.

3. Table of Citations. Here the writer lists all of the authorities used and indicates where they are cited in the brief. The table of citations demands great technical care and thus produces the most headaches and eyestrain in briefwriting. Citations must be accurate and complete, and must include all of the information required by the bluebook. All page numbers, volume numbers, underlining, parentheses, brackets, and spacing should be checked carefully. Consult the tables of citations from the *Bell-Wesley v. O'Toole* briefs for examples of proper form for typewritten citations.

The list of citations may be divided into at least three sections: cases, statutes, and miscellaneous. Entries should be arranged alphabetically within each category. "Miscellaneous" can be subdivided into "Restatements," "Treatises," etc., if need be. Recheck your moot court rules to make sure that you have not exceeded the allowable number of cited authorities.

E. PITFALLS TO AVOID: FACT ANEMIA AND THE AGATHA CHRISTIE SYNDROME

There are two frequently diagnosed syndromes encountered in many first attempts at appellate briefwriting. First is Fact Anemia. Rather than argue the facts of her case, the advocate producing a fact-anemic brief will devote long paragraphs to the historical evolution of a current legal standard. Extended quotations often accompany this affliction. Befuddled judges may glance at the cover page of the brief to make sure that they have not accidentally picked up a law review article.

This style is simply not persuasive. Direct references to the facts of the case are essential ingredients of your arguments. The court must apply principles of law to the particular facts of the case. You should attempt to incorporate facts into every paragraph of the argument.

The second commonly observed syndrome is the Agatha Christie, Esq., malady. The writer gives clues, and the court, as if it were reading a murder mystery, must wait in suspense until reaching the conclusion. Many briefwriters seem reluctant, after weeks of scrupulous analysis and insights of intuition, to give away the punchline.

This is counterproductive. Stating the conclusion early and often is a must for a persuasive brief. Since the stuff of many appellate dramas is less compelling than the plots of most detective stories, you have to tell the reader why to keep reading. Otherwise, you may lose him on page five, long before he reaches your brilliantly crafted climax on page seven.   In short, the destination of your argument should appear at the beginning.   Tell the court what you are going to say, say it, and then conclude by summarizing what you have said. An inverse pyramid is much more persuasive than suspense.

F. SO YOU'RE OVER THE PAGE LIMIT, AND OTHER EDITING TIPS

Many have said that there is no good writing, only good rewriting.   Whether or not you are indeed over the page limit, virtually any first draft of anything can use a little judicious editing.   You can make your moot court adviser's work a little less difficult by preempting some of the tricks of the advising trade.

1. Rewriting.   The "What do you mean?" trick goes something like this.   Adviser points to a particularly convoluted two-page paragraph, raises eyebrows, and asks advisee, "What do you mean to say here?"   Advisee pauses, then gives a cogent two-sentence explanation.   Adviser says "Good. Why don't you write that?"   Don't give your adviser such satisfaction.   Conduct this test on your own, and deconvolute.

The "slash and burn" technique can also be preempted.   Certain patterns of words can instinctively be crossed out wherever they appear, without any loss of meaning.   Examples of such terms are: "It can be argued," "It seems that," "Cases have clearly held," and "It is beyond argument that."   Just leave them out.   Your prose will be that much clearer, stronger, and shorter.

2. Polishing.   You can tighten your brief by eliminating string cites, summarizing lengthy quotations, putting subsidiary points in footnotes, and not devoting scarce space to arguing uncontroverted points of law.   Polish your vocabulary.   Eliminate unnecessary adverbs.   Change passive constructions to active wherever you have not intentionally used the passive voice.   Jettison the legalese.

Finally, editing gives you a good excuse to proofread.   Judges are not going to decide cases based on animosity inspired by a misspelling.   However, as Judge Pell of the Seventh Circuit once noted, "[t]here is a gnawing feeling on occasion that the obviousness of the uncorrected errors indicates that the brief, having not been read for those errors, may be equally unreliable in substance, reasoning, or its analysis of authorities."[2]   Do not let your credibility flounder because of an unnoticed typographical error.

[2.]   Pell, Read Before Signing, 66 A.B. A.J. 977 (1980).

G. SAMPLE BRIEFS: BELL–WESLEY v. O'TOOLE

Sample briefs for both parties in the case of *Bell-Wesley v. O'Toole* begin on the following page. The brief for the plaintiff-appellants, Rebecca and Scott Bell-Wesley, is intended to be rather strident in tone. The brief for the defendant-appellee, Dr. Stephen O'Toole, adopts a cooler, more reasoned style.

IN THE SUPREME COURT OF THE
STATE OF AMES

Civil Action No. 83-2004

SCOTT AND REBECCA BELL-WESLEY, Plaintiff-Appellants

v.

DR. STEPHEN O'TOOLE, Defendant-Appellee

BRIEF FOR THE PLAINTIFF-APPELLANTS

Jane E. Harvey
Attorney for the
Plaintiff-Appellants

Argument: March 23, 1984
Ames Courtroom
7:30 p.m.

*

TABLE OF CONTENTS

Page

TABLE OF AUTHORITIES ii

QUESTIONS PRESENTED 1

STATEMENT OF THE CASE 1

ARGUMENT 4

I.   THE BELL-WESLEYS' WRONGFUL BIRTH CLAIM MUST BE RECOGNIZED
     BECAUSE DR. O'TOOLE'S NEGLIGENT STERILIZATION OPERATION
     AND SPERM COUNT CAUSED THEM SUBSTANTIAL PHYSICAL,
     EMOTIONAL, AND FINANCIAL INJURY 4

II. DR. O'TOOLE MUST BE HELD LIABLE TO THE BELL-WESLEYS FOR
     ALL OF THE DAMAGES FLOWING FROM HIS REPEATED NEGLIGENCE. 9

     A. The Bell-Wesleys Should Be Compensated For All Their
        Injuries, Including Sterilization Costs, Pre-natal and
        Post-natal Medical Expenses, Emotional and Physical
        Pain and Suffering, Financial Sacrifices, and the Costs
        of Raising Their Unplanned Child 9

     B. The "Benefits Rule" Does Not Warrant Offset of the
        Bell-Wesleys' Damages Because Any Benefits Received
        Affect a Different Interest Than That Harmed By
        O'Toole's Negligence 13

     C. The Bell-Wesleys Were Not Obligated to Abort Their
        Child, to Place Him for Adoption, or to Submit to
        Amniocentesis Because They Were Required Only to Take
        Reasonable Steps to Mitigate Their Damages 15

CONCLUSION 17

i

*

TABLE OF AUTHORITIES

CASES   <u>Page</u>

Boone v. Mullendore, 416 So. 2d 718 (Ala. 1982) 9

Clapham v. Yanga, 102 Mich. App. 47, 300 N.W.2d 727 (1981) . 16

Custodio v. Bauer, 251 Cal. App. 2d 303, 59 Cal.
     Rptr. 463 (1967) 10, 11, 12

Griswold v. Connecticut, 381 U.S. 479 (1965) 7

Hartke v. McKelway, 707 F.2d 1544 (D.C. Cir. 1983),
     cert. denied, 104 S.Ct. 425 (1983) 5, 11, 14

Kingsbury v. Smith, 122 N.H. 237, 442 A.2d 1003 (1982) . 12, 14

Ochs v. Borelli, 187 Conn. 253, 445 A.2d 883 (1982) . . 7, 11

Rivera v. State, 94 Misc. 2d 157, 404 N.Y.S.2d 950
     (1978) 7, 16

Roe v. Wade, 410 U.S. 113 (1973) 7

Shelley v. Kraemer, 334 U.S. 1 (1948) 7

Sherlock v. Stillwater Clinic, 260 N.W.2d 169
     (Minn. 1977) 5, 10, 12, 14

Stills v. Gratton, 55 Cal. App. 3d 698, 127 Cal. Rptr. 652
     (1976) 13

Troppi v. Scarf, 31 Mich. App. 240, 187 N.W.2d 511
     (1971), lv. denied, 385 Mich. 753 (1971) 6, 7, 16

Ziemba v. Sternberg, 45 A.D.2d 230, 357 N.Y.S.2d 265 (1974). 16

MISCELLANEOUS

Comment, Judicial Limitations on Damages Recoverable for the
     Wrongful Birth of a Healthy Infant, 68 Va. L. Rev. 1311
     (1982) 14

Kashi, The Case of the Unwanted Blessing: Wrongful Life,
     31 U. Miami L. Rev. 1409 (1977) 15

McCormick, Handbook on the Law of Damages § 35 (1935) . . . 15

Note, Wrongful Birth: A Child of Tort Comes of Age,
     50 U. Cin. L. Rev. 65 (1981) 5

  Page

Note, Wrongful Conception: Who Pays for Bringing Up Baby?,
    47 Fordham L. Rev. 418 (1978-79) 8

W. Prosser, Law of Torts (4th ed. 1971) 4, 10

Restatement (Second) of Torts, § 918 (1972) 15

Restatement (Second) of Torts, § 920 (1972) 13, 14, 15

iii

QUESTIONS PRESENTED

Should traditional tort principles be defied by denying recovery to parents who suffered serious injuries from a doctor's negligent performance of a vasectomy and of a sperm count resulting in the birth of an unplanned, unwanted child?

Should a doctor whose negligent performance of a sterilization and of a sperm count inflicted numerous injuries upon an innocent couple be held responsible for the full extent of his negligence, including the medical costs, the physical and emotional pain and suffering, and the extensive financial costs associated with the birth of a child?

STATEMENT OF THE CASE

Appellants Rebecca and Scott Bell-Wesley brought this civil action in the Superior Court for the State of Ames to recover for the injuries resulting from defendant Dr. Stephen O'Toole's negligence in the performance of a vasectomy and in subsequent testing and consultation. The injuries the Bell-Wesleys suffered are those associated with the unwanted conception and birth of their child, Frank Michael Bell. The Bell-Wesleys appeal the Superior Court's failure to recognize their wrongful birth claim.

1

Rebecca and Scott Bell-Wesley are established professionals who live in Holmes, Ames. Scott works as an architect in the Holmes City Planning Department. Rebecca, an attorney, accepted a position as First Assistant Attorney General of the State of Ames in 1981, shortly after her husband's vasectomy. (R.11)

Before January 1983, Rebecca Bell-Wesley gave birth to three congenitally deformed children, each of whom died in infancy. (R.1) Dr. O'Toole informed the Bell-Wesleys that there was a seventy-five percent probability that any child they conceived would suffer the same deformity. With this knowledge, Scott and Rebecca made a conscious decision to lead a childless life. (R.1) Although they could have adopted a child, they instead chose to devote their time and energy to their careers and each other. On October 16, 1981, the defendant performed a vasectomy on Scott Bell-Wesley to insure that the couple would remain childless permanently. (R.2) Three months later O'Toole performed a sperm count on Scott Bell-Wesley and informed him that the operation had rendered him sterile. (R.2)

In April 1982, Rebecca Bell-Wesley discovered that she was pregnant. The Bell-Wesleys refused to abort the child on moral grounds. (R.7) They also chose not to undergo amniocentesis. (R.6) On January 4, 1983, Rebecca Bell-Wesley gave birth to a healthy baby boy, Frank Michael Bell. (R.2) The Superior Court concluded as a matter of fact that the defendant's negligence

2

caused this birth; Dr. O'Toole failed to sever the tubes of Scott's vas deferens properly, and compounded his negligence by misperforming the sperm count. (R.9)

The Bell-Wesleys brought this medical malpractice action to recover the substantial injuries caused by O'Toole's carelessness. While Rebecca and Scott love Frank deeply, his conception and birth have nonetheless caused them severe emotional, physical, and financial harm. In addition to the pain and the substantial medical expenses related to the pregnancy, the Bell-Wesleys suffered considerable trauma from the conception and birth of a child whom they expected to be deformed. (R.2,3) Frank's birth has forced the Bell-Wesleys to alter their lives dramatically. (R.7) Both parents have lost, and will continue to lose, time and wages from their careers in order to care for the child. (R.8) After deciding to remain childless, Rebecca decided to devote more time to her career and accepted an important promotion with the Attorney General's office. Her salary increased from $24,000 to $40,000 per year. Rebecca's leave of absence in connection with the pregnancy has placed her job in jeopardy. (R.4) The financial and emotional costs of raising Frank present the Bell-Wesleys with a formidable burden.

While the Superior Court recognized O'Toole's repeated acts of negligence, it refused to recognize the Bell-Wesleys' claim for wrongful birth. Instead, the court limited the recovery to $500, covering only the medical costs, pain and suffering, and

3

loss of consortium immediately associated with the vasectomy.
The Bell-Wesleys appeal to this court for recognition of their
wrongful birth claim, seeking to recover for all the injuries
caused by defendant's negligence.

ARGUMENT

I.   THE BELL-WESLEYS' WRONGFUL BIRTH CLAIM MUST BE RECOGNIZED
      BECAUSE DR. O'TOOLE'S NEGLIGENT STERILIZATION OPERATION
      AND SPERM COUNT CAUSED THEM SUBSTANTIAL PHYSICAL,
      EMOTIONAL, AND FINANCIAL INJURY.

Basic common law tort principles mandate recognition of
the Bell-Wesleys' wrongful birth claim against Dr. O'Toole.
The couple's cause of action is based upon the elements which
constitute any negligence claim: duty, negligence, proximate
cause, and injury. See W. Prosser, Law of Torts § 30 (4th ed.
1971). As the trial court found, on two separate occasions Dr.
O'Toole breached a professional duty of care toward the
Bell-Wesleys. (R.7) O'Toole's negligent performance of Scott's
vasectomy and of the sperm count proximately caused the
conception and birth of the Bell-Wesleys' unplanned child.
(R.7) While the trial court denied that a healthy child's
birth could be accompanied by any injury to its parents, the
Bell-Wesleys have in fact met with serious physical, financial,
and emotional injuries. They have also suffered the violation
of their constitutionally protected right to self-determination
in the realm of family planning. The policies that underpin
every tort cause of action, deterring tortfeasors and
compensating their victims, compel recognition of the

4

Bell-Wesleys' wrongful birth claim. The Bell-Wesleys' claim is "indistinguishable from an ordinary medical malpractice action." Sherlock v. Stillwater Clinic, 260 N.W.2d 169, 174 (Minn. 1977) (failed vasectomy resulting in birth of healthy, unplanned child created cause of action against negligent physician, with damages allowed for pregnancy, birth, and childrearing). More than sixty state and federal cases have recognized wrongful birth claims. Note, Wrongful Birth: A Child of Tort Comes of Age, 50 U. Cin. L. Rev. 65 (1981).

For Rebecca and Scott, the trial court's antiquated notion that the birth of a child is always a "blessing" is meritless. Frank's conception and birth substantially injured the Bell-Wesleys' physical, emotional, and financial well-being. Rebecca's pregnancy was accompanied by the severe emotional trauma which, after the birth of three deformed children, the Bell-Wesleys sought to avoid through sterilization. Moreover, the couple's decision to undergo an irreversible sterilization operation demonstrated that they rejected traditional attitudes towards procreation. While they could have adopted children, Rebecca and Scott instead chose to pursue a childless lifestyle, recognizing that parenthood entails numerous costs, burdens, and responsibilities which may outweigh its attendant joys. Where a couple elects not to have children, it should be presumed that the birth of a child does not benefit them. Hartke v. McKelway, 707 F.2d 1544, 1552 (D.C. Cir. 1983) (failed tubal ligation, resulting in birth of healthy child,

created wrongful birth claim against the physician), <u>cert.</u>
<u>denied</u>, 104 S.Ct. 425 (1983). The Bell-Wesleys reassessed
their opportunities and resources and radically altered their
beliefs about the purposes and goals of their marriage. They
decided to devote more time to each other and to their careers,
only to have their expectations shattered as a result of
O'Toole's repeated negligence.

Policy considerations dictate that these injuries to Scott
and Rebecca be compensated like those in any other medical
malpractice action. The general sentiment of the American
public today is one of respect for family planning decisions.
Tens of millions employ contraceptives daily to prevent the
birth of children; these persons, "by their conduct, express
the sense of the community." <u>Troppi v. Scarf</u>, 31 Mich. App.
240, 253, 187 N.W.2d 511, 517 (1971) (negligent filling of a
birth control prescription with tranquilizers created a
wrongful birth cause of action against the pharmacist, with
damages recoverable for pregnancy, birth, and childrearing
costs), <u>lv. denied</u>, 385 Mich. 753 (1971). While judicial
exceptions to standard tort law doctrines should "express the
manifest will of the people," <u>Troppi</u>, 31 Mich. App. at 252, 187
N.W.2d at 516, the trial court's declaration that a child's
birth is always a "blessing" reflects only the crusading
paternalism of a bygone era.

The Bell-Wesleys' determination that Scott would undergo a
vasectomy was an intimate, personal family planning matter that

6

falls within the zone of privacy and self-determination
protected by the Constitution. See Griswold v. Connecticut,
381 U.S. 479 (1965); Roe v. Wade, 410 U.S. 113 (1973). Rebecca
and Scott had a fundamental right to determine not to have
children. Rivera v. State, 94 Misc. 2d 157, 162, 404 N.Y.S.2d
950, 953 (1978) (negligent tubal ligation operation created
malpractice cause of action for damages for medical expenses,
pain and suffering, and costs of raising an unwanted child).
O'Toole's repeated negligence thwarted their exercise of this
right. When a doctor's negligence "results in the birth of an
unwanted child, a substantial interference with the fundamental
rights of the parents occurs," and the courts should recognize
its significance. Id., 94 Misc. 2d at 162, 404 N.Y.S.2d at
953. Public policy prohibits allowing an exception to tort
liability where "the impact of such an exception would impair
the exercise of a constitutionally protected right." Ochs v.
Borrelli, 187 Conn. 253, 256, 445 A.2d 883, 885 (1982)
(negligent tubal ligation).[1]

---

1 Refusal by Ames' courts to recognize the Bell-Wesleys'
wrongful birth claim could itself be seen as a violation of the
couple's right to self-determination. At least one court has
held that "since the State may not infringe upon this right, it
may not constitutionally denigrate the right by completely
denying protection provided as a matter of course to like
rights." Troppi, 31 Mich. App. at 253-254, 187 N.W.2d at 517;
Rivera, 94 Misc. 2d at 162, 404 N.Y.S.2d at 954. Cf. Shelley
v. Kraemer, 334 U.S. 1 (1948) (court enforcement of racially
restrictive covenant is state action).

7

Negligent physicians like Dr. O'Toole must not be allowed to escape the consequences of their carelessness. Recognition of a wrongful birth cause of action is necessary to deter negligence and to insure a proper standard of medical care. Faced with a blameworthy defendant, O'Toole, and his innocent victims, the Bell-Wesleys, it is in society's best interest to compensate the victims for their losses, rather than to grant the tortfeasor immunity. Fairness requires that Dr. O'Toole pay for the consequences of his wrongful behavior, rather than force his innocent victims to absorb the costs of his negligence. See generally Note, Wrongful Conception: Who Pays for Bringing Up Baby?, 47 Fordham L. Rev. 418 (1978-79).

Recognition of the Bell-Wesleys' wrongful birth claim would in no way denigrate the value of Frank Bell's life. Frank is not an item of damage in this suit. The issue is not Frank or the love his parents feel for him, but the negligence that led to his birth, denied the Bell-Wesleys the opportunity to lead their chosen lifestyle, and imposed upon them burdens that they were entitled to avoid through sterilization.

Recognition of the Bell-Wesleys' claim will not result in psychological harm to a child who discovers that he was unplanned. Frank could easily be protected from this unlikely event by keeping the names involved in this action confidential. Most importantly, recovery by the Bell-Wesleys will inure to Frank's emotional benefit, since it will relieve "the economic pressure of raising an unexpected child and

8

permit the parents to concentrate on giving the child the love and care he or she needs." Boone v. Mullendore, 416 So. 2d 718, 724-25 (Ala. 1982) (recognizing wrongful birth claim for birth of healthy but unplanned child) (Faulkner, J., concurring).

Rebecca and Scott Bell-Wesley have demonstrated all of the elements that constitute medical malpractice, and are entitled to recover for the extensive injuries caused by defendant's negligence. Any exception from standard tort law that immunized O'Toole would victimize Frank Bell's innocent parents and contravene public policies favoring family planning and self-determination, discouraging careless behavior, and redressing harms.

II. DR. O'TOOLE MUST BE HELD LIABLE TO THE BELL-WESLEYS FOR ALL OF THE DAMAGES FLOWING FROM HIS REPEATED NEGLIGENCE.

    A. The Bell-Wesleys Should Be Compensated For All Their Injuries, Including Sterilization Costs, Pre-natal and Post-natal Medical Expenses, Emotional and Physical Pain and Suffering, Financial Sacrifices, and the Costs of Raising Their Unplanned Child.

Rebecca and Scott Bell-Wesley are entitled to recover for all of the injuries resulting from Dr. O'Toole's defective sterilization operation and sperm count, including their pain and suffering, emotional trauma, lost earnings, the costs of raising Frank, and the sacrifice of their chosen lifestyle. The standard formula for tort remedies should apply to this wrongful birth claim as it does to any medical malpractice

9

action; Dr. O'Toole must be held liable for all injuries flowing naturally and foreseeably from his repeated negligence. See W. Prosser, supra p. 4, at § 43. The obvious consequences of a negligently performed sterilization are the conception and birth of an unplanned child and the associated costs of pregnancy, birth, and upbringing. See Custodio v. Bauer, 251 Cal. App. 2d 303, 322-23, 59 Cal. Rptr. 463, 476-77 (1967) (valid wrongful birth claim arising from negligent tubal ligation).

The Bell-Wesleys should recover for each of the injuries which O'Toole has inflicted upon them because the fundamental aim of tort recovery is to place the victim in the same position she would have been in had the tort never occurred. The Superior Court's failure to acknowledge the Bell-Wesleys' cause of action has left uncompensated significant emotional and economic harms. The medical expenses associated with Rebecca's pregnancy and Frank's birth are costs that the Bell-Wesleys would not have incurred but for O'Toole's malfeasance. Pre- and post-natal medical expenses are generally awarded in wrongful birth actions. See, e.g., Sherlock, 260 N.W.2d at 175; Custodio, 251 Cal. App. 2d at 322-23, 59 Cal. Rptr. at 476-77. Moreover, Rebecca endured great physical pain and both Scott and Rebecca suffered loss of consortium in connection with the pregnancy, injuries for which they are entitled to further damages. See Sherlock, 260 N.W.2d at 175.

10

The Bell-Wesleys suffered acute mental anguish after learning that Rebecca was pregnant. Scott and Rebecca had experienced three other pregnancies, each resulting in deformed children who died shortly after birth. O'Toole himself had informed them that any future pregnancy was seventy-five percent likely to have similarly tragic results. Thus, for over eight months, the Bell-Wesleys lived in fear that Rebecca would give birth to another deformed child. Their damage award should reflect the mental suffering O'Toole's negligence inflicted. See Ochs, 187 Conn. at 257, 445 A.2d at 886 (recognizing that fear of the birth of a handicapped child is a compensable injury); Hartke, 707 F.2d at 1555 (mother's anxiety about unborn child's potential deformity merited damage award).

Both Scott and Rebecca have lost and will continue to lose valuable time and earnings in their chosen careers. Rebecca's leave of absence from her position as Assistant Attorney General has deprived her of valuable career experiences necessary to her professional development and may have jeopardized her job. (R.11) As the Superior Court noted, the defendant's negligence has profoundly altered the Bell-Wesleys' lifestyle. (R.7) Frank's birth and the resulting responsibilities have greatly curtailed the financial and emotional freedom the couple enjoyed. The Bell-Wesleys should be compensated for this economic and emotional strain. See Custodio, 251 Cal. App. 2d at 322-24, 59 Cal. Rptr. at 476-77.

11

O'Toole's tortious conduct has thrust the extensive financial burden of raising a child upon Scott and Rebecca. They seek to recover not for Frank's life, but for the diminution in family wealth which necessarily resulted from his birth. See id., 251 Cal. App. 2d at 324, 59 Cal. Rptr. at 477. The costs of raising Frank "are a direct financial injury to the parents, no different in immediate effect than the medical expenses resulting from the wrongful conception and birth of the child." Sherlock, 260 N.W.2d at 175. Government studies of the economic costs of raising children provide a reasonable basis for judicial assessment of the extent of this injury. (R.4) Therefore, Rebecca and Scott should recover for the costs of rearing Frank.

Recovery for all emotional and pecuniary costs is necessary to compensate the Bell-Wesleys for the full extent of their injuries and to hold O'Toole liable for the complete consequences of his negligence. This recovery is not disproportionate to the actions of Dr. O'Toole; the doctor could easily have limited his liablity by taking the simple step of providing proper post-operative care. Full recovery by wrongful birth claimants is necessary to sufficiently deter negligence in performing vasectomies. Courts must assess doctors for the full costs of their malfeasance in order to provide adequate incentives for safe, effective medical procedures. See Kingsbury v. Smith, 122 N.H. 237, 242, 442 A.2d 1003, 1005 (1982) (failure to recognize wrongful birth

12

claims would "[dilute] the standard of professional conduct and expertise in the area of family planning").

    B.   The "Benefits Rule" Does Not Warrant Offset of the Bell-Wesleys' Damages Because Any Benefits Received Affect a Different Interest Than That Harmed By O'Toole's Negligence.

The extensive damages to the Bell-Wesleys should not be offset by any benefits they received through the birth of their unplanned child. Courts have sometimes permitted such an offset, purporting to rely upon the "benefits rule" of section 920 of the Restatement (Second) of Torts. See, e.g., Stills v. Gratton, 55 Cal. App. 3d 698, 707-09, 127 Cal. Rptr. 652, 658-59 (1976). Section 920 provides:

> When the defendant's tortious conduct has caused harm to the plaintiff or to his property and in doing so has conferred a special benefit to the interest of the plaintiff that was harmed, the value of the benefit conferred is considered in mitigation of damages, to the extent that this is equitable.

Restatement (Second) of Torts, § 920 (1972) (emphasis added). The birth of an unplanned, unwanted child undoubtedly confers some benefits upon the Bell-Wesleys. Nonetheless, these benefits cannot mitigate the Bell-Wesleys' injuries because they involve interests distinct from those harmed by O'Toole's misconduct. The equitable considerations embodied in the benefits rule bar offsetting these benefits against the Bell-Wesleys' damage award.

The emotional benefits the Bell-Wesleys received through the "joys of parenthood" are of an entirely different nature and kind

13

than the financial injuries and the pain and suffering inflicted on them by O'Toole's negligence. Rebecca and Scott's deep love for Frank does not negate the fact that his birth was neither planned nor desired. Their affection for Frank will not provide the Bell-Wesleys with the money to cover his expenses or replace the time and energy diverted from their careers. When "[p]roperly applied in the wrongful birth context, the benefit rule would allow the recovery for emotional harm to be offset only by an emotional benefit, the recovery for an economic harm to be offset only by an economic benefit, and so on." Comment, Judicial Limitations on Damages Recoverable for the Wrongful Birth of a Healthy Infant, 68 Va. L. Rev. 1311, 1326 (1982). The examples provided in the Restatement indicate that the drafters supported distinguishing between emotional, physical, and pecuniary interests when applying the benefits rule. Restatement (Second) of Torts, § 920, comment b, illustrations 4 and 6 (1972). The Bell-Wesleys' love for Frank will not heal the injuries to their economic and professional situation. At most, the "joys" of parenthood could offset only the emotional burden directly associated with raising Frank. In no event should any benefits be offset against the injuries Scott and Rebecca experienced up to and including the time of Frank's birth, since they could receive no benefit from the child before he was born. See Sherlock 260 N.W.2d at 175-76 (allowing offset of benefits only against rearing costs); Kingsbury, 122 N.H. at 243, 442 A.2d at 1005 (1982) (denying offset against sterilization and pregnancy costs); see also Hartke, 707 F.2d at 1557 n.16.

14

Offsetting the benefits of parenthood against the Bell-Wesleys' injuries would pervert the equitable result contemplated by section 920. Rebecca and Scott elected to exercise their fundamental right of self-determination to <u>avoid</u> the joys of parenthood. The Bell-Wesleys' loss of control over their lifestyle which resulted from O'Toole's careless misconduct cannot be compensated by any benefits associated with raising Frank. Section 920's purpose is to keep the victim from recovering more than the harm incurred, ". . . and not to permit the tortfeasor to force a benefit or him against his will." Restatement (Second) of Torts, § 920, comment f (1972). <u>See also</u> Kashi, <u>The Case of the Unwanted Blessing: Wrongful Life</u>, 31 U. Miami L. Rev. 1409, 1415 (1977) (characterizing doctor-conferred benefits in wrongful birth cases as "officious intermeddling"). O'Toole cannot be permitted to escape liability for the serious injuries he has inflicted upon the Bell-Wesleys because he has forced upon them a "benefit" which they obtained a vasectomy specifically to avoid.

    C.   <u>The Bell-Wesleys Were Not Obligated to Abort Their Child, to Place Him for Adoption, or to Submit to Amniocentesis Because They Were Required Only to Take Reasonable Steps to Mitigate Their Damages</u>.

O'Toole could not require the Bell-Wesleys to undergo amniocentesis, to abort Frank, or to place him up for adoption. The couple was obligated only to take reasonable steps to mitigate the damages caused by O'Toole's negligence. <u>See</u> Restatement (Second) of Torts, § 918; McCormick, <u>Handbook on the Law of Damages</u> § 35

15

(1935). Abortion, adoption, and amniocentesis go far beyond reasonable mitigation of damages.

O'Toole has no right to insist that Rebecca "have the emotional and mental makeup of a woman who is willing to abort" her child. Troppi, 31 Mich. App. at 260, 187 N.W.2d at 520. Rebecca and Scott declined to abort their child on moral grounds. (R.7) A rule of law which ignored their beliefs and required Rebecca to have an abortion "would constitute an invasion of privacy of the grossest and most pernicious kind." Rivera, 94 Misc. 2d at 163, 404 N.Y.S.2d at 954. "The right to have an abortion may not automatically be converted to an obligation to have one" in order to mitigate wrongful birth damages. Ziemba v. Sternberg, 45 A.D.2d 230, 233, 357 N.Y.S.2d 265, 269 (1974).

Requiring Scott and Rebecca to place Frank up for adoption would ignore the natural bonds of parenthood established during the nine month term of pregnancy. See Clapham v. Yanga, 102 Mich. App. 47, 61, 300 N.W.2d 727, 733 (1981) (familial ties held to render mitigation by adoption unreasonable even where claimants were grandparents who voluntarily took and cared for the child). While the Bell-Wesleys had made a conscious choice not to conceive a child, their natural affection for Frank renders placement for adoption unreasonable. To force the Bell-Wesleys to part with another child after the loss of their first three children would compound the emotional trauma caused by defendant's carelessness.

The Bell-Wesleys' decision to forego amniocentesis was reasonable in light of the surrounding circumstances. Amniocentesis

16

involves analysis of amniotic fluid obtained by the insertion of an eight-inch needle into the mother's abdomen. We now know that submission to this painful process would have revealed that the unplanned child was normal. When Scott and Rebecca made their decision, however, they knew only that it was highly probable that the child was deformed. (R.1) They were unwilling to abort the child in any circumstance. Therefore, submission to the test was likely only to increase the couple's suffering by confirming that Rebecca would give birth to a deformed child. The Bell-Wesleys behaved reasonably in avoiding this additional trauma.

CONCLUSION

Dr. O'Toole's repeated negligence caused the Bell-Wesleys substantial physical, financial, and emotional injuries that were left uncompensated by the Superior Court. Therefore, this court should reverse the judgment of the Superior Court and award full recovery to Rebecca and Scott Bell-Wesley.

Respectfully submitted,

Jane E. Harvey

Jane E. Harvey
Attorney for Plaintiff-Appellants

17

*

IN THE SUPREME COURT OF THE
STATE OF AMES

Civil Action No. 83-2004

SCOTT AND REBECCA BELL-WESLEY, Plaintiff-Appellants

v.

DR. STEPHEN O'TOOLE, Defendant-Appellee

BRIEF FOR THE DEFENDANT-APPELLEE

D. Nathan Neuville
Attorney for the Appellee

Argument: March 23, 1984
Ames Courtroom
7:30 p.m.

*

TABLE OF CONTENTS

                                                            Page

TABLE OF CITATIONS ii

QUESTIONS PRESENTED 1

STATEMENT OF FACTS 1

ARGUMENT 3

I.   THE COURT SHOULD NOT CREATE A WRONGFUL BIRTH CAUSE OF
     ACTION FOR THE BELL-WESLEYS BECAUSE THE BIRTH OF THEIR
     HEALTHY, NORMAL SON AFTER THEY SOUGHT STERILIZATION
     SOLELY TO AVOID A DEFORMED CHILD WAS A BLESSING, NOT AN
     INJURY 3

II. THE BENEFITS RESULTING FROM FRANK BELL'S BIRTH AND HIS
     PARENTS' FAILURE TO MITIGATE DAMAGES PRECLUDE THE
     BELL-WESLEYS FROM RECOVERING DAMAGES EXCEEDING THOSE
     AWARDED BY THE SUPERIOR COURT. 10

     A.   The Benefits the Bell-Wesleys Derive From the Birth
          of Their Son Outweigh All Costs Associated With His
          Birth and Rearing, Barring Recovery For Those Costs
          Under the Benefits Rule. 10

     B.   The Bell-Wesleys' Failure to Mitigate Their Damages
          Through the Reasonable Steps of Amniocentesis and
          Adoption Forecloses Further Recovery 15

CONCLUSION 17

*

TABLE OF CITATIONS

CASES

Page

Beardsley v. Wierdsma, 650 P.2d 288 (Wyo. 1982) 11

Betancourt v. Gaylor, 136 N.J. Super. 69, 344 A.2d 336
   (1975) 6

Christensen v. Thornby, 192 Minn. 123, 255 N.W. 620 (1934) . 5

Cockrum v. Baumgartner, 99 Ill. App. 3d 271,
   425 N.E.2d 968 (1982), rev'd 95 Ill. 2d 193,
   447 N.E.2d 385 (1983) 4, 7, 11, 14

Coleman v. Garrison, 349 A.2d 8 (Del. 1975). 5

Griswold v. Connecticut, 381 U.S. 479 (1965) 6, 7

Hartke v. McKelway, 707 F.2d 1544 (D.C. Cir. 1983),
   cert. denied, 104 S.Ct. 425 (1983) 9, 12

Ocns v. Borrelli, 187 Conn. 253, 445 A.2d 883 (1982). 5

Public Health Trust v. Brown, 388 So. 2d 1084 (Fla. App.
   1980). 5, 12

Rieck v. Medical Protective Co., 64 Wis. 2d 514, 219
   N.W.2d 242 (1974) 8, 9

Roe v. Wade, 410 U.S. 113 (1973) 6, 7

Sherlock v. Stillwater Clinic, 260 N.W.2d 169 (Minn.
   1977) 6, 8, 11

Terrell v. Garcia, 496 S.W.2d 124 (Tex. Civ. App. 1973),
   cert. denied, 415 U.S. 927 (1974) 11, 15

Troppi v. Scarf, 31 Mich. App. 240, 187 N.W.2d 511
   (1971), lv. denied, 385 Mich 753 (1971) 10, 12, 14

University of Arizona Health Services Center v.
   Superior Court of Maricopa County, 136 Ariz. 579,
   667 P.2d 1294 (1983) 10, 12, 14

Wilbur v. Kerr, 275 Ark. 239, 628 S.W.2d 568 (1982) 7

Intro. to Advocacy 4th Ed.—4

MISCELLANEOUS

Page

Comment, Judicial Limitations on Damages Recoverable for the
  Wrongful Birth of a Healthy Infant, 68 Va. L. Rev. 1311
  (1982) 14

W. Prosser, Law of Torts (4th ed. 1971) 3

Restatement (Second) of Torts, § 918 (1972) 15

Restatement (Second) of Torts, § 920 (1972) 10, 13

QUESTIONS PRESENTED

Should a "wrongful birth" cause of action be created for the birth of a normal child to parents who had long wanted a child and who sought sterilization solely to avoid bearing a deformed child?

If a "wrongful birth" claim is created, should the damages claimed by the parents be offset by the extensive benefits they derive from their healthy child or reduced due to the parents' failure to mitigate damages through the reasonable measures of amniocentesis and adoption?

STATEMENT OF FACTS

Appellants Rebecca and Scott Bell-Wesley brought suit in the Superior Court of the State of Ames against Dr. Stephen O'Toole, an established Ames physician, seeking damages for the birth of a healthy, normal child following an unsuccessful sterilization.

Mr. and Ms. Bell-Wesley are a successful professional couple residing in Holmes, Ames. Scott Bell-Wesley is an architect, and Rebecca Bell-Wesley is an Assistant Attorney General for the State of Ames. On three occasions before the January 1983 birth of their son, Frank Michael Bell, the

1

Bell-Wesleys had attempted to start a family. Each time, however, Ms. Bell-Wesley gave birth to a congenitally deformed infant that died within six months of birth. (R.1) Dr. O'Toole informed the Bell-Wesleys that there was a seventy-five percent chance that any child they conceived would suffer the same deformity. For the sole purpose of avoiding the conception of another deformed child, the Bell-Wesleys decided to have Dr. O'Toole sterilize Mr. Bell-Wesley. (R.7)

On October 16, 1983, Dr. O'Toole performed a vasectomy on Mr. Bell-Wesley. (R.8) After a follow-up sperm count, Dr. O'Toole mistakenly informed Mr. Bell-Wesley that he was sterile. (R.9) Six months after the vasectomy, Ms. Bell-Wesley discovered that she was pregnant. Ms. Bell-Wesley refused to undergo amniocentesis, a simple procedure that would have revealed that the fetus she carried was normal in every respect. (R.6,8) On January 4, 1983, Ms. Bell-Wesley gave birth to a healthy, normal son, Frank Michael Bell. (R.7) While they characterize Frank as an "unwanted" child, the Bell-Wesleys have declined to put him up for adoption. (R.8)

Although they profess great love for their son, the Bell-Wesleys brought suit against Dr. O'Toole, claiming to be injured by Frank's birth. The Bell-Wesleys seek damages of approximately $140,000 to cover items such as injury to their "lifestyle" and the financial and emotional costs of raising Frank. (R.2-3) Judge Nancy Llewenstein of the Superior Court found that the vasectomy was unsuccessful and that the sperm

2

count was negligently performed. (R.9) The court awarded the

Bell-Wesleys damages for the out-of-pocket costs, pain and

suffering, and loss of consortium incident to the vasectomy.

Id. The court refused to allow a wrongful birth cause of

action for the costs incident to Rebecca's pregnancy and the

birth and rearing of Frank Bell, holding that the benefits to

the Bell-Wesleys of this healthy, normal child outweigh any

attendant costs. (R.10) The Bell-Wesleys appeal the Superior

Court decision.

ARGUMENT

I. THE COURT SHOULD NOT CREATE A WRONGFUL BIRTH CAUSE OF ACTION
    FOR THE BELL-WESLEYS BECAUSE THE BIRTH OF THEIR HEALTHY,
    NORMAL SON AFTER THEY SOUGHT STERILIZATION SOLELY TO AVOID A
    DEFORMED CHILD WAS A BLESSING, NOT AN INJURY.

The Bell-Wesleys cannot recover for "wrongful birth" because

Frank Bell's birth was a blessing, not an injury. The Bell-

Wesleys have failed to demonstrate an indispensable element of

their tort claim: a legally recognizable injury. W. Prosser,

Law of Torts § 30 (4th ed. 1971). While the Bell-Wesleys

characterize their son's birth as a harm, many jurisdictions

have denied that a healthy child's birth can ever be an injury

to its parents. The birth of a normal son to parents who

procured a vasectomy solely to avoid having a deformed child is

not an injury, even under the rationales adopted by courts

recognizing wrongful birth claims. Furthermore, a number of

3

serious public policy concerns preclude labeling Frank's birth an injury.

The Bell-Wesleys have suffered no injury. For years they yearned for a healthy child like Frank. Before Frank's birth, the Bell-Wesleys had tried to start a family on three separate occasions, only to see each attempt result in the birth of a deformed, short-lived child. (R.1) The Bell-Wesleys abandoned their hopes of having a family only when Dr. O'Toole informed them that it was highly probable that any child they conceived would suffer the same deformity. Scott Bell-Wesley obtained a vasectomy solely to avoid the birth of another deformed child. (R.7) The birth of a healthy child, especially in light of the deaths of their earlier children, is a great benefit to the Bell-Wesleys. The Bell-Wesleys proclaim that they love their child deeply, yet they now style Frank's birth an "injury." It is difficult to believe that they would make this characterization absent the prospect of pecuniary gain. As Judge Llewenstein concluded, under these circumstances Frank's birth can only be seen as a blessing. (R.10)

The notion that the Bell-Wesleys were injured by the birth of a healthy child "offends . . . fundamental values attached to human life." Cockrum v. Baumgartner, 95 Ill. 2d 193, 198, 447 N.E.2d 385, 388 (1983) (refusing to recognize a cause of action for the birth of a healthy child after a negligent vasectomy). Many courts, reasoning that "the value of a human life outweighs any 'damage' which might be said to follow from the fact of

4

birth," have held that a healthy child's birth is never an injury, regardless of the circumstances. <u>Coleman v. Garrison</u>, 349 A.2d 8, 13 (Del. 1975); <u>see also</u> <u>Public Health Trust v. Brown</u>, 388 So. 2d 1084 (Fla. App. 1980). Because the Bell-Wesleys actually desired a healthy child, this Court need not go so far as to proclaim that a child's birth can never be an injury in order to conclude that the value of life forbids labeling Frank's birth an injury.

The circumstances of Frank's birth stand in sharp contrast to the situations in which wrongful birth claims have been recognized because the Bell-Wesleys have escaped the injury they sought to avoid. Courts have sometimes recognized wrongful birth claims where the parents, like the Bell-Wesleys, sought sterilization for eugenic or therapeutic reasons. However, they have done so only where the child's birth has resulted in the deformity or other physical injury the parents intended to guard against. <u>Compare</u>, <u>e.g.</u>, <u>Ochs v. Borrelli</u>, 187 Conn. 253, 445 A.2d 883 (1982) (recognizing claim for birth of child with mild orthopedic defects after negligent sterilization operation), <u>with</u> <u>Christensen v. Thornby</u>, 192 Minn. 123, 255 N.W. 620 (1934) (where the purpose of sterilization was to prevent physical risk to the mother, the birth, without complications, of a healthy infant was not actionable). The Bell-Wesleys sought only to avoid the birth of a fourth deformed child; they cannot recover for the birth of the healthy, normal child they always wanted.

5

The Bell-Wesleys did not obtain a vasectomy because they felt they could not afford a child or because they wished to limit the size of their family, two other situations in which courts have recognized wrongful birth claims. Some courts have permitted recovery for wrongful birth where a child is born after a non-therapeutic sterilization because the child represents the very thing its parents sought to avoid: an economic drain on family resources or a simple increase in family size. See, e.g., Sherlock v. Stillwater Clinic, 260 N.W.2d 169 (Minn. 1977) (sterilization sought in order to limit family size after birth of seventh child); Betancourt v. Gaylor, 136 N.J. Super. 69, 74, 344 A.2d 336, 339 (1975) (parents sought to avoid expense of additional child). Scott and Rebecca Bell-Wesley, however, decided upon sterilization for purely therapeutic reasons. These two professionals sought for years to expand their family and are well able to provide for their son. No court has ever permitted recovery for wrongful birth under such circumstances.

The Bell-Wesleys' constitutional privacy rights under Griswold v. Connecticut, 381 U.S. 479 (1965), and Roe v. Wade, 410 U.S. 113 (1973), are not at issue in this lawsuit. Contra Appellants' Brief at 6-7. Roe and Griswold establish privacy rights which protect the Bell-Wesleys only against "state action" or government intrusion. See, e.g., Roe, 410 U.S. at 153. There has been no state action against the Bell-Wesleys; Dr. O'Toole is a private individual, not a government agent.

6

The Bell-Wesleys' privacy rights are also uninfringed because the couple procured a vasectomy for therapeutic reasons, not for the purpose of limiting family size. Roe and Griswold articulate the right of parents to control their family's size. The Bell-Wesleys, however, have consistently sought to increase their family's size, not to limit it.

Recognizing the Bell-Wesleys' cause of action would undermine important notions of parental responsibility and risk causing Frank severe emotional trauma. The prospect of financial gain will induce parents to proclaim publicly that their child's birth was an injury. Encouraging such claims will adversely affect family structure. To recover for wrongful birth, parents would have to "demonstrate not only that they did not want the child," but also that "the child remains an uncherished, unwanted burden." Cockrum, 95 Ill. 2d at 202, 447 N.E.2d at 390. Parents will resent and be alienated from children that they have been encouraged to view as injuries; they will accept their obligations towards such children grudgingly. When a child such as Frank learns that he was unwanted, that his parents felt injured by his birth, and that they were unwilling to pay for his expenses themselves, he will suffer serious emotional injury. Our society has not become so "sophisticated" as to "dismiss [the] emotional trauma [of a child] as nonsense." Wilbur v. Kerr, 275 Ark. 239, 244, 628 S.W.2d 568, 571 (1982) (denying revovery for the expense of raising an unwanted, healthy child).

7

The recovery the Bell-Wesleys seek is not commensurate with Dr. O'Toole's culpability. See Rieck v. Medical Protective Co., 64 Wis. 2d 514, 518-19, 219 N.W.2d 242, 244-45 (1974) (excessive burden on physician and other public policy concerns preclude recovery for birth of unwanted child). The costs of raising Frank to adulthood, estimated by the Bell-Wesleys at over $100,000, (R.4), are astronomical in comparison to those involved in a vasectomy, a low-cost operation performed in the doctor's own office. The goal of deterrence has already been adequately served by the Superior Court's award of damages and, more importantly, by the accompanying injury to Dr. O'Toole's professional reputation. To go beyond the trial court's award and assess liability which is grossly disproportionate to Dr. O'Toole's negligence will result in the practice of "defensive" medicine and in increased sterilization costs. Faced by the prospect of devastatingly disproportionate liability and dramatically increased insurance costs, physicians may counsel against sterilization when the operation is in their patient's best interest. Physicians will pass their increased costs on to their patients by charging greater fees for sterilization, denying a socially valuable family planning option to low-income patients.[1]

---

[1] Ironically, some courts have justified liability for wrongful birth by noting that public policy favors contraception. See, e.g., Sherlock, 260 N.W.2d at 175; see also Appellants' Brief at 5. As this analysis demonstrates, imposition of liability will have a detrimental effect upon the

8

Because the Bell-Wesleys did not procure sterilization for financial reasons, allowing them to recover the costs of raising Frank would grant them a "windfall." See Hartke v. McKelway, 707 F.2d 1544, 1553-55 (D.C. Cir. 1983), cert. denied, 104 S.Ct. 425 (1983); Rieck, 64 Wis. 2d at 518-19, 219 N.W.2d at 244-45. The Bell-Wesleys will enjoy every benefit, tangible and intangible, associated with raising a healthy child whom they adore. Meanwhile, Dr. O'Toole and, via insurance, the rest of society, will be forced to bear all of the costs intertwined with these benefits. The Bell-Wesleys never sought to avoid these costs and are fully capable of bearing them. Recognition of their wrongful birth claim would unjustly enrich the Bell-Wesleys.

Creating a wrongful birth cause of action for the Bell-Wesleys would threaten the emotional well-being of children, have deleterious effects upon family structure, and impose excessive liability upon physicians. It might be possible to ignore these concerns where the wrongful birth claimants could not provide for their child's needs or where the child was unhealthy. The Bell-Wesleys, however, are financially capable and have become the parents of the healthy child they desired. To find that the birth of this normal child injured a couple that sought sterilization only to avoid a deformed child would be a radical deviation from the common law, including that

---

goal of universally attainable contraception.

of states recognizing wrongful birth claims. The Bell-Wesleys'

attempt to fashion a wrongful birth cause of action out of

these circumstances must be rejected.

II. THE BENEFITS RESULTING FROM FRANK BELL'S BIRTH AND HIS
    PARENTS' FAILURE TO MITIGATE DAMAGES PRECLUDE THE
    BELL-WESLEYS FROM RECOVERING DAMAGES EXCEEDING THOSE
    AWARDED BY THE SUPERIOR COURT.

   A. The Benefits the Bell-Wesleys Derive From the Birth of
      Their Son Outweigh All Costs Associated With His Birth
      and Rearing, Barring Recovery For Those Costs Under the
      Benefits Rule.

   Even if the Bell-Wesleys' claim is recognized, they are entitled

to no further damages because the benefits accruing to them from

Frank's birth outweigh any purported injuries. The benefits rule of

the Restatement (Second) of Torts provides:

> Where the defendant's tortious conduct has
> caused harm to the plaintiff or to his property
> and in so doing has conferred upon the
> plaintiff a special benefit to the interest
> which was harmed, the value of the benefit
> conferred is considered in mitigation of
> damages, where this is equitable.

Restatement (Second) of Torts, § 920 (1972). Every

jurisdiction recognizing wrongful birth claims employs the

benefits rule to offset the benefits of parenthood against any

injuries. See, e.g., University of Arizona Health Sciences

Center v. Superior Court of Maricopa County, 136 Ariz. 579,

584-86, 667 P.2d 1294, 1299-1301 (1983); Troppi v. Scarf, 31

Mich. App. 240, 254-57, 187 N.W.2d 511, 517-18 (1971), lv.

denied, 385 Mich. 753 (1971). Numerous courts have held that

10

the benefits of a healthy, normal child outweigh the costs of
rearing her as a matter of law. The Bell-Wesleys' own
evaluation of the costs and benefits of parenthood, evident
from their repeated attempts to have a healthy child,
demonstrates that Frank's birth was, on balance, a benefit to
them. Any further damage award would unjustly enrich the
Bell-Wesleys at Dr. O'Toole's expense.

Frank's birth will bring his parents all the joy and
satisfaction normally associated with parenthood. The
equitable principle embodied in the benefits rule requires that
the Bell-Wesleys' damages be offset by the "value of the
child's aid, comfort, and society which will benefit the
parents for the duration of their lives." Sherlock, 260 N.W.2d
at 176. While these benefits are great, they are also largely
intangible and elude financial calculation. To place a dollar
value upon these benefits would be to denigrate the value of
the child's life. Many courts have recognized that these
benefits cannot and should not be subject to judicial
assessment; they have concluded that the incalculable benefits
received by the parents outweigh the costs of raising a healthy
child as a matter of law. See Beardsley v. Wierdsma, 650 P.2d
288, 293 (Wyo. 1982) (any attempt to measure these benefits
would be a "misplaced attempt to put a specific dollar value on
a child's life"); see also Cockrum, 95 Ill. 2d at 200-01, 447
N.E.2d at 388-89; Terrell v. Garcia, 496 S.W.2d 124, 128 (Tex.
Civ. App. 1973), cert. denied, 415 U.S. 927 (1974).

Even if the benefits of a healthy child were not held to outweigh the costs in every case, the Bell-Wesleys' demonstrated desire for a healthy child requires a holding that the benefits predominate in this case. Correct application of the benefits rule requires examination of all the circumstances surrounding the parents' wrongful birth claim. Troppi, 31 Mich. App. at 254-57, 187 N.W.2d at 518-19. When the Bell-Wesleys conceived each of their three deceased children they had determined that the joys of parenthood exceeded the emotional and financial costs of pregnancy, birth, and child-rearing. Nothing indicates that the Bell-Wesleys ever altered their evaluation; they sought sterilization solely because they feared the birth of a fourth deformed child. (R.7) The purpose for which the parents sought sterilization is the most telling evidence of whether, on balance, the child's birth actually damaged the couple. See University of Arizona, 136 Ariz. at 585, 667 P.2d at 1300; Hartke, 707 F.2d 1544. Because the Bell-Wesleys' purpose was to avoid a deformed child, the birth of their normal son has not damaged them.

The Bell-Wesleys' subsequent behavior indicates that they do not feel injured by Frank's existence. They stress their love for Frank, Appellants' Brief at 3, 14, and decline to place him for adoption. See Public Health Trust, 388 So. 2d at 1086 (failure to place the child for adoption indicates that the parents are benefited by keeping the child). Moreover,

12

they have not altered their lifestyle greatly since Scott
Bell-Wesley's vasectomy. The only visible change in the
Bell-Wesleys' circumstances is Rebecca's new position. Ms.
Bell-Wesley had held this job for less than six months when she
discovered she was pregnant. Her affection for Frank
demonstrates that she did not become so caught up in her new
position during this short period that she abandoned her desire
for a child. This couple desperately wished to have a healthy
child of their own; Frank's arrival was a long-hoped-for
blessing.

The Bell-Wesleys' desire for a child is hardly surprising,
since child-rearing will place a relatively slight burden upon
them. As an architect and a lawyer, Mr. and Ms. Bell-Wesley
will have no difficulty supporting Frank financially. The
Bell-Wesleys have no other children, so Frank's birth will not
deprive any siblings of parental care or support. For years
the couple has been fully prepared to accept the economic and
emotional costs of raising a child, yet the list of damages
that they now claim is no more than a catalogue of the costs
normally associated with bearing and raising a child. The
Bell-Wesleys' own assessment of parenthood establishes that the
benefits of Frank's birth outweigh these costs.

Recognition of the enormous benefits associated with
Frank's birth is not precluded by the benefits rule's
requirement that the benefits be "to the interest of the
plaintiff which was harmed." Restatement (Second) of Torts,

13

§ 920 (1972). Courts applying this equitable principle in
wrongful birth cases generally offset all of the costs involved
by all of the benefits. See, e.g., Troppi, 31 Mich. App. at
255, 187 N.W.2d at 518; see also Comment, Judicial Limitations
on Damages Recoverable for the Wrongful Birth of a Healthy
Infant, 68 Va. L. Rev. 1311 (1982). While it may be
conceptually possible to distinguish between the Bell-Wesleys'
economic and emotional interests in Frank's birth, the
practical reality is that these interests are inextricably
intertwined. See University of Arizona, 136 Ariz. at 584 &
n.4, 667 P.2d at 1299 & n.4; Troppi, 31 Mich. App. at 255, 187
N.W.2d at 518. There is no jurisdiction in which these
interests are separated in applying the benefits rule to a
wrongful birth claim.[2] The equitable rule against unjust
enrichment, embodied in the benefits rule, compels the offset
of all the benefits of Frank's birth against all of the costs.

Furthermore, Frank's presence benefits the interests the
Bell-Wesleys claim were harmed. While they allege injury to
their "childless lifestyle," their persistent attempts at
childbearing demonstrate that Frank enhances their lifestyle.
Frank will even provide future financial benefits; "a child is

---

[2] The only case in which economic and emotional interests
were distinguished when applying the benefits rule in a
wrongful birth context was subsequently reversed. See Cockrum
v. Baumgartner, 99 Ill. App. 3d 271, 425 N.W.2d 968 (1982),
rev'd 95 Ill. 2d 193, 447 N.E.2d 385 (1983).

14

some security for the parents' old age." <u>Terrell</u>, 496 S.W.2d at
128. Failure to offset the benefits of Frank's birth based on
a "same interest" rationale will unjustly enrich the
Bell-Wesleys, producing a result antithetical to the benefits
rule.

    B. <u>The Bell-Wesleys' Failure to Mitigate Their Damages</u>
       <u>Through the Reasonable Steps of Amniocentesis and</u>
       <u>Adoption Precludes Further Recovery</u>.

The Bell-Wesleys are also barred from any further recovery
because of their failure to mitigate their damages. They may
not recover damages for injuries resulting from an
unintentional tort when they could have avoided that harm
through reasonable effort. Restatement (Second) of Torts,
§ 918 (1972). Amniocentesis and adoption were reasonable steps
that would have eliminated virtually all of the damages the
Bell-Wesleys seek to recover. The Bell-Wesleys cannot force
Dr. O'Toole to compensate them for injuries they could have
avoided by fulfilling their duty to mitigate damages.

Amniocentesis would have eliminated any emotional trauma
Mr. and Ms. Bell-Wesley experienced due to fear that their
child would be deformed. The trial court determined that this
safe, simple procedure would have revealed that Frank was
healthy and free of deformity. (R.8) Under the circumstances,
having amniocentesis performed was the most reasonable measure
for the Bell-Wesleys to take. Even had Frank been deformed,
knowledge of this would have caused the Bell-Wesleys no more

emotional trauma than that caused by the uncertainty suffered
before Frank's birth. On the other hand, the discovery that
Frank was normal would have prevented any emotional suffering.
Given the ease with which the Bell-Wesleys could have avoided
emotional trauma, that element must be eliminated from any
evaluation of the Bell-Wesleys' damages.

If the Bell-Wesleys were actually burdened more than they
were benefited by Frank's birth, the reasonable step to
mitigate their damages was to put the child up for adoption.
To justify an award of damages to the Bell-Wesleys, it would be
necessary to find that the personal ties between parent and
child which society normally presumes to be of great value,
were insufficiently valuable to the Bell-Wesleys to offset the
costs of bearing and raising a child. See discussion supra, p.
10. If the Bell-Wesleys place so little value upon the
parent-child relationship that a normal, healthy child
represents a net burden to them, it was unreasonable for them
to refuse to put the child up for adoption. Frank would be
better off in a home with adoptive parents who cherish their
relationship with him and who regard themselves as better off
with than without him. By their own estimation, the
Bell-Wesleys would be better off as well. If it is
unreasonable to ask the Bell-Wesleys to give Frank Bell up for
adoption, it is because they do, in fact, derive a greater
benefit than burden from parenthood.

16

The Bell-Wesleys' failure to mitigate their damages by undergoing amniocentesis or placing Frank for adoption precludes them from recovering the damage which could have been avoided by these steps.

CONCLUSION

For the foregoing reasons, the judgment of the Superior Court should be affirmed.

Respectfully submitted,

D. Nathan Neuville
Attorney for the Appellee

17

Chapter V

GENERAL RULES OF STYLE AND CITATION OF AUTHORITIES

The questions of why and when to cite authorities in a brief have already been discussed. This chapter is designed to indicate the functions that the form of citation serves and to suggest the basic rules governing form. These rules are based on *A Uniform System of Citation* (13th ed. 1981), published by the Harvard Law Review Association, subject to modification where brief writing citation requirements differ from the needs of other types of legal work. That book (commonly called the "bluebook"), which contains rules governing matters not covered in this chapter, is a useful reference work.

Rules presented in this chapter pertain directly to citations in briefs. Citations to authority are placed in the text of the brief and are not put in footnote form.

This chapter deals in Part A with the general rules that govern the writing of a brief. The remaining parts of the chapter deal with the technicalities relating to the citation of authorities in the brief. Part B takes up the necessary elements of information which a citation must contain. Part C deals with the indication of the purpose and weight of citations, and the treatment of multiple authorities cited for the same point. The actual form of citations is dealt with in Part D (Cases), Part E (Statutes and Constitutions), and Part F (Secondary Authorities).

For the most part, citations in this chapter are only illustrative of proper form. They do not refer to actual cases.

A. GENERAL RULES OF STYLE

1. ABBREVIATIONS

Many abbreviations permitted in citations are not acceptable when used in the body of the brief or in the Table of Citations. For abbreviations in case names, see Part D.1.c. of this chapter.

Well-known statutes and agencies may be designated by initials after the full name has been written out once. The periods are omitted unless the initials designate a case reporter. "The National Labor Relations Board has done commendable work. At its inception, the NLRB was not . . . ." Names of states and the "United States" must not be abbreviated.

2. **CAPITALIZATION**

    a. **Capitalization of Specific Words.** The following words are capitalized only in the following situations:

        "Act"—when referring to a specific act: the National Labor Relations Act . . . the Act.

        "Bill"—when part of a proper name given in full.

        "Circuit"—when used with the circuit number. First Circuit.

        "Code"—when referring to a specific code: the 1939 and 1954 Codes.

        "Constitution"—when referring to the United States Constitution or to any constitution in full. Exception: federal constitution. Do not capitalize the parts of the Constitution: fifth amendment, article III. But: Bill of Rights.

        "Court"—when naming any court in full; otherwise, only when referring to the United States Supreme Court: the Supreme Court of Illinois; the [state] supreme court; the court of appeals; the Court of Appeals for the Fifth Circuit.

        "Federal"—only when the word it modifies is capitalized.

        "Government"—when it is an unmodified noun standing alone meaning the United States government.

        "Justice"—when referring to a Justice of the United States Supreme Court.

        "National"—only when the word it modifies is capitalized.

        "Rule"—when part of a proper name given in full.

        "State"—when the word it modifies is capitalized.

        "Statute"—when part of a proper name given in full.

    b. **Capitalization of Famous Old Statutes and Rules.** The names of famous old statutes and rules such as the Statute of Frauds and the Rule Against Perpetuities are customarily capitalized. The statute of limitations is not capitalized.

    c. **Words Denoting Groups or Officeholders.** These (such as the Congress, the Senate, the Agency, the Commission, the President) are capitalized when referring to a specific federal government body, office, or official. Adjectival forms of these words are not capitalized (congressional hearing, the agency hearing, etc.)

3. **ITALICIZATION AND UNDERLINING**

    Italicization is indicated on a typewriter by underlining and is used in the following circumstances:

a. Case Names. The names of both parties and the "v." between should be underlined. Italicization is used also in abbreviated references to cases. "The *Jones* case held . . . ." The Latin words in a case name are also underlined. *In re McLaughlin; Ex parte Savin.*

b. Introductory Signals. All introductory signals are italicized.

c. Foreign Words and Phrases. Italicization of foreign words and phrases is determined by the usage of the second edition of *Merriam-Webster New International Dictionary.* Words to be italicized are indicated in that work (and its abridged editions) by a prefix of two vertical parallel bars.

> (1) *Foreign words always italicized: ex parte, ex rel., i.e., in re, inter alia, inter se, passim, quaere, semble, sic., sub nom.,* and *supra.*

> (2) *Foreign words not italicized include:* ad hoc, a fortiori, amicus curiae, bona fide, certiorari, de novo, dictum, ipso facto, mandamus, per curiam, per se, prima facie, pro rata, quo warranto, res judicata, stare decisis, and subpoena (and its modifiers).

4. NUMBERS, SYMBOLS, AND DATES

Numbers under 100 should always be written out in the body of a brief, except when relating to a statistical study, or when used in a date. The month of a date should always be written out.

The word "section" must be spelled out, unless part of a citation. The word "percent" is also spelled out in the text of the brief. Dollar signs may be used in the brief, except when beginning a sentence.

5. QUOTATIONS

Quotations under 50 words in length, set off by quotation marks, are incorporated in the regular flow of the text. Those more than 50 words in length must be indented and single spaced. Indented quotations are not set off by quotation marks.

a. Placement of Quotation Marks. Periods and commas should always be placed inside quotation marks. All other punctuation marks should be placed outside the quotation marks unless they are part of the material quoted.

b. Omissions From Quotations. Omission of material from a quotation must be indicated. All omissions of material from sentences must be indicated, as well as omissions of sentences and paragraphs from quotations. Sentences and paragraphs are not "omitted" unless they originally fell *within* the quoted material.

(1) *Short quotations.* Omission of matter before or after a quotation of a phrase or less need not be indicated, unless it would be misleading to not indicate the omission.

(2) *Clarification of noun, pronoun or verb.* When a bracket insertion clarifies a noun or pronoun or changes the tense or number of a verb, the corresponding omission need not be indicated.

(3) *Omission at the beginning of a sentence.* The omission of language at the beginning of a quoted sentence is indicated by capitalizing and placing in brackets the first letter of the first word of the quoted section.

(4) *Omission of the middle of a sentence.* Omitting language from the middle of a sentence is indicated by inserting three spaced periods set off by a space before the first period and after the last period.

(5) *Omission at the end of a sentence.* Omitting language at the end of a sentence is indicated by inserting four spaced periods set off by a space before the first period.

(6) *Omission from the middle of a quotation.* The omission of language after the end of a quoted sentence followed by the rest of the quotation is indicated by retaining the period at the end of the quoted sentence and inserting three spaced periods set off by a space before the first period and after the last period. If the omission is from the start of a new quoted paragraph, the spaced periods are indented. When an entire paragraph is omitted, four spaced and indented periods are placed where the paragraph would have been.

c. Alterations in Quotations.

(1) *Added italics or omitted footnotes.* Alterations of the quotation, such as the addition of italics to some portion of it or the omission of footnotes are indicated by comments in parentheses at the end of the quotation's citation, and should read: "(emphasis added)" or "(footnotes omitted)."

(2) *Change of letter.* A change in a quotation from a lower case letter to a capital is indicated by bracketing the letter.

(3) *Supplementary or explanatory words.* Supplementary or explanatory words inserted in a quotation must be enclosed in brackets. (On typewriters without bracket symbols, brackets may be made with the slash bar and the underlining bar.)

d. Page Numbers of Quoted Materials. Indicate the page upon which a quotation begins and, if it continues to another page, the page on which it ends. This may be done in the sentence introducing the quoted material. With a short quotation, the citation may appear as a sentence following the quotation. Where there is a lengthy, single-spaced, and indented quotation, the citation may appear at the end of the quotation. Preferred practice puts the citation within parentheses if the citation follows an indented quotation. The citation need not be put in parentheses if it appears as the first nonindented material after the indented quotation.

6. TECHNICAL WORDS OF REFERENCE

a. "Infra" and "Ibid." In briefs, use *"id."* to cite to the immediately preceding authority. Do not use *"infra."*

b. "Supra." *Supra* is only appropriate for material other than cases or statutes. It is used only when the complete citation of the material appeared previously in the same general discussion. *Introduction to Advocacy, supra.* If necessary to refer to a particular page of a citation previously given in the same general discussion, use the following form: *Introduction to Advocacy, supra* at 61.

c. References to the Record. References to the record of a case should follow the cited material with the letter "R." and the page number in parentheses as (R. 17). This is not underlined.

d. References to Footnotes. References to footnotes in a work are made by using the letter "n." *E.g.,* 1 S. Williston, *Sales* 63 n. 7, 64 nn. 9–11 (rev. ed. 1948).

e. References to Briefs. References to the briefs in a case should appear as follows: Brief for Appellee at 20; Brief for Plaintiff at 7.

7. THE TABLE OF CITATIONS

a. Citation of Cases. The rules of style for citation of cases in the body of the brief also apply in the Table of Citations section. The names of cases are underlined in the Table of Citations section just as they are in the body. The cases are listed in alphabetical order. For examples of proper citation form for a typewritten brief, see the tables of citation in the sample briefs in *Bell-Wesley v. O'Toole* at pp. 55 and 79.

b. Citation of Statutes.

   (1) *Abbreviations.* Statute names should be written out more completely in the Table of Citations section. In the body, greater abbreviation is permitted. Maine Revised Statutes ch. 2, § 1 (1930).

(2) *Location.* Remember that statutes are primary authorities and should be listed immediately following cases in the Table of Citations section.

c. **Citations of Secondary Authorities.** All secondary authorities are grouped under the heading "Miscellaneous" in the Table of Citations. They should be listed here in alphabetical order.

8. A NOTE ON THE SPACING OF CITATIONS

There are many different rules concerning the spacing of citations in legal materials. Courts, publishers, law firms, law reviews, and other legal writers may follow different schemes, and may even be inconsistent within any one document. This internal inconsistency is to be avoided.

A Uniform System of Citation (13th ed. 1981) suggests a system which is followed in the sample briefs in *Bell-Wesley v. O'Toole.* Single capitals are closed up, *except* when an entity is abbreviated by widely recognized initials and combination of those initials with others would be confusing. *E.g.,* Yale L.J.; Nw. U.L. R.; *But:* U.C.L.A. L. Rev.

For the purposes of these rules, individual numbers are treated as single capitals. *E.g.,* F.2d; N.W.2d; N.Y.S.2d; *But:* So. 2d; Cal. 2d.

Because of the nature of printing process, the typewritten briefs in this book should be consulted for the spacing of citations, rather than the text. They begin on p. 51.

B. NECESSARY ELEMENTS OF INFORMATION

Citations must convey certain essential information. They must (1) identify the authority, (2) indicate where it is found, (3) indicate the "author" of the authority, (4) indicate the date of the authority, and (5) indicate the purpose for which the authority is cited and the weight to be attached to it.

1. **Identification of Authority.** The case name must be stated. Where several different cases are decided with one opinion, or the case name is unusually long, see Part D.1. of this chapter for the proper way of giving this essential information in the briefest form.

2. **Where the Authority May Be Found.** The "location" of the authority is the publication in which it has been printed. When the authority is a judicial decision, it is customary to refer to both the official and the unofficial reporters, if they are available; an exception to this rule exists where the case is decided by the Supreme Court of the United States or by lower federal courts. Both volume and page numbers are necessary.

If the authority is an article, the volume of the periodical in which it appears and the number of the page on which it begins are necessary. A treatise citation should contain the volume, section and sometimes the topic in which it can be found. Other books are cited similarly except that the author's name and page number are used.

3. Indication of "Author." Counsel must indicate the person or persons who wrote or stand behind the printed words on which he relies. If it is a case, the citation must identify precisely the court by which it was decided. This will usually be accomplished by reference to the official reporter in which the opinion appears, since most official reporters cover only the highest court of the state. For instance, *Snow v. Wragg*, 303 Mass. 264, 131 N.E. 206 (1900), shows that the Supreme Judicial Court of Massachusetts decided the case, for it is the only court reported in the Massachusetts Reports. However, some official reporters cover more than the highest court. Almost all unofficial reporters cover more than one court. If the case is in one of this class of reporters, the court must be indicated in parentheses. If the identity of the court is obvious from name of the reporter, the court of decision need not be indicated even if it is not the highest court in the jurisdiction. Thus: *Van Allen v. Semmi*, 24 App. Div. 2d 316, 217 N.Y.S.2d 408 (1965) but *Muir v. Alsup*, 221 Misc. 498, 50 N.Y.S.2d 897 (Sup. Ct. 1944).

If the authority is a treatise, the author must be given. With such authorities as the *American Law of Property*, it is customary to name the editor in parentheses. For more exact information, see the section dealing with citations to secondary authorities (Part F *infra*).

4. Date. The year in which the case was decided, the article written, the statute enacted, or the treatise published must be given. It may have a direct bearing on the weight which the court will attach to the authority since social conditions or policy may well have changed since that time.

5. Indication of Purpose and Weight of the Citation. It is extremely important to inform the court, through the citation form, of the citation's purpose and to indicate what importance (weight) is to be attached to it. This is accomplished through the use of introductory signals and parenthetical information.

The absence of signal before a citation indicates to the court that the authority cited directly upholds the proposition for which it is cited. It is imperative that counsel master the various signals.

Information as to the weight of the authority is given by the presence or absence of explanatory remarks in parentheses after the case. If one uses a case where the court gave its view on an issue, even though it was not necessary for decision, then he must inform the court that it is dictum. Thus: *Passman v. Anderson,* 343 N.Y. 204, 126 N.E. 675 (1959) (dictum). The explanatory comment in parentheses after the case may contain various other desirable comments such as an indication of the judge who wrote the opinion. Absence of any explanatory data affirmatively indicates certain information to the court. For a more complete discussion, see the section dealing with parentheticals indicating weight (Part C.3. *infra*).

C. INDICATION OF PURPOSE AND WEIGHT; ORDER FOR MULTIPLE AUTHORITIES

Proper citation of all authorities (cases, treatises, statutes, etc.) involves indicating the purpose of the citation through its form—that is, informing the judge of the logical relationship which the cited authority bears to the proposition advanced (support, contradiction, etc.). The citation must also inform the judge of the weight which is to be attached to the authority—that is, whether it is holding, dictum or concurring opinion, etc.

Below is a description of some of the relationships of citation to text which can be indicated by the presence or absence of introductory signals and by the use of particular signals.

Groups of citations are given in "sentences." A new sentence of citations is introduced with a capitalized, introductory signal even though the sentence may contain more than one signal. Within a sentence each citation except the last is followed by a semicolon. The last one is followed by a period. All authorities supporting a point are placed in the same sentence. Authorities opposing the point are placed in a separate one. The authorities and signals are placed in the order listed below. Signals which are capitalized even when they do not begin a sentence are indicated below; all signals must be italicized unless a typewriter is used, in which case they must be underlined.

1. SIGNALS INDICATING PURPOSE

a. Authorities Supporting the Point. When authorities support the proposition advanced, various degrees of support are indicated by the absence of any express signal and by the use of *"e.g.," "accord," "see," "see also,"* and *"cf."*

(1) [No signal] No express signal is used when the case directly holds the proposition of law for which it is cited.

The absence of an express signal indicates that it is a holding, or identifies the source of a quotation.

(2) *"E.g.,"* Use *"e.g.,"* when there are more examples other than the ones cited but citation to them would not be helpful. This signal should be preceded by a comma when used in combination with other signals and is always followed by a comma. *E.g., Howarth v. Rice,* 408 F.2d 246 (2d Cir. 1969). *See, e.g., Gould v. Smith,* 212 Mass. 17, 218 N.E.2d 842 (1965).

(3) *"Accord,"* *"Accord,"* may be used when the cited authority directly supports the statement in the text, but in a slightly different way than the authority first cited. Its use is most appropriate when the cases are directly in point but the text quotes from or states the facts of one of the cases. Similarly, the law of one jurisdiction may be cited as in accord with that of another jurisdiction if the law is exactly the same. *Accord, Maguire v. McCurdy,* 325 U.S. 6 (1945). Or, after the principal case: *Bordwin v. Ames,* 98 U.S. 64 (1878); *accord, Chase v. Freeman,* 300 U.S. 27 (1937). Note that *"accord,"* is always followed by a comma.

(4) *"See"* *"See"* indicates that the asserted opinion or conclusion will be suggested by an examination of the cited authority rather than that the opinion or conclusion is stated by the authority. *See Gordon v. Cushing,* 251 F.2d 8 (3d Cir.1955).

(5) *"See also"* Use *"see also"* to cite additional cases that directly support a point when the main case has already been discussed. Follow the citation with a parenthetical explanation of the material's relevance. *See also Roberts v. Stern,* 234 F. 12 (D.C. Cir. 1938); *LeClair v. Presser,* 84 Or. 714, 402 P.2d 102 (1965).

(6) *"Cf."* If the cited case or other source material expresses a proposition which is only analogous to the point under discussion, but lends some support to the statement, conclusion, or opinion in the brief, use *"cf."* before the citation. *Cf. Smith v. Abrams,* 162 Mo. 220, 140 S.W. 518 (1925).

b. Authorities Opposing the Point. When authorities oppose the proposition advanced, various degrees of opposition are indicated by the use of *"Contra,"* *"But see"* and *"But cf."*

(1) *"Contra,"* Precede the citation with *"Contra,"* when citing cases holding the opposite of a proposition. *"Contra,"* is followed by a comma. This is comparable to when *"[no signal]"* would be used for support. This signal always

begins a new sentence. *Contra, Areeda v. Steiner,* 243 U.S. 21 (1917).

(2) *"But see"* and *"But cf."* The citation *"But see"* precedes a case not squarely contradictory to the proposition, but which casts doubt upon it. If the case is only analogous, use *"But cf." "But see"* and *"But cf."* are analogous to *"see"* and *"cf."* After the first citation to an authority which opposes the proposition being advanced, the *"But"* is dropped from all the "opposing citation" signals which follow in that sentence. *But see Wilson v. Lodge,* 245 U.S. 18 (1918); *cf. Roosevelt v. Taft,* 300 U.S. 200 (1940). Note that these signals always begin a new sentence unless the first signal is *"contra."*

c. Authority Not Lending Support to Proposition. When the cited authority is broader in scope than, or develops a question analogous to, discussion in text without lending support to the proposition asserted, *"see generally"* indicates the cited authority can be profitably compared with the proposition. As with other signals, a parenthetical explanation helps the reader understand the case's relevance. *See generally* Brylawski, *Welfare Systems and Poverty in the United States,* 68 Yale L.J. 812 (1966). *"See generally"* always begins a new sentence of citations.

d. Comparing Authorities With One Another. To compare one cited case with another case, rather than with the text of the brief, use *"Compare . . . with . . . . " Compare Vogel v. Stroh,* 205 F.2d 811 (2d Cir. 1959), *with Britton v. Buchanan,* 204 F.2d 367 (3d Cir. 1959).

2. ORDER OF AUTHORITIES

Multiple authorities on the same point must be cited in the order explained below. However, it is seldom wise to give more than two or three authorities for a particular point, especially in moot court competition.

a. Order of Signals. In a citation string, citations are grouped in an order dependent upon the introductory signal preceding them. Each signal or absence of a signal applies to all citations following it until another signal is given or the sentence ends. Signals are given in the order in which they are described in the preceding section, that is, with citations preceded by no signal coming first, signals indicating support next, all signals indicating opposition next, and other signal types following. A sentence only contains authority that is either supporting, opposing or neither. If both supporting and opposing citations are used, two sentences must be used. Within a multiple citation of authorities on the same point, signal groups are given in the following order:

(1) Holding (no signal) (2) *e.g.,* (3) *accord,* (4) *see* (5) *see also* (6) *cf.* (7) *Contra,* (8) *But see* (9) *But cf.* (10) *See generally*

Note the use of citation sentences in the following example. Fed. R. Civ. P. 9(a); *accord,* N.J.R. Civ. P. 9(a); *see Ehrlich v. Grossman,* 215 N.E.2d 919 (Mass. 1966); *cf.* N.Y.R. Civ. Prac. 97 (McKinney 1962). *Contra, Arp. v. Grenier,* 234 F.2d 425 (5th Cir. 1956) (rule 9(a) invalid); *see* 2 J. Moore, *Federal Practice* ¶ 9.02 (2d ed. 1948); *cf.* Iowa R. Civ. P. 101. *See generally Filvoroff v. Wertheimer,* [1953] 1 Q.B. 646.

b. Order within Signals. Within each introductory signal group, cases are given first, statutes second, and secondary authority last. Specific order within these groups is given below.

(1) *Cases.* Counsel should first cite the strongest authority by the most persuasive court. All other things being equal, cases are arranged according to the courts issuing the cited opinion (prior history, etc., is irrelevant to the order). All the United States courts of appeals are treated as one court for this purpose, as are all district courts. Within each court, order is given chronologically, with the most recent decisions first.

Federal: (a) United States Supreme Court decisions.

(b) courts of appeals.

(c) district courts.

(d) other federal courts.

(e) administrative agencies.

State: (f) state court decisions (in alphabetical order of states, then by rank of court within the state).

(g) state agencies (in alphabetical order of states, then alphabetically within each state).

Foreign: (h) foreign courts, common law followed by civil-law (in alphabetical order of countries, then by rank of court within each country).

Note: Within groups of cases preceded by the same introductory signal, all citations to holdings precede all citations to (1) alternative holdings, (2) concurring or dissenting opinions, and (3) dicta. These latter three classifications are treated as a single group and no special order among them is required.

(2) *Statutes and Constitutions.* Subject to the rule that the strongest authority should be cited first the following order should be used:

(a) Constitutions (U.S. and then alphabetically by state)

(b) Federal statutes

    (i) currently in force, in order of U.S.C. title

    (ii) currently in force but not in U.S.C. (most recent first)

    (iii) rules of evidence and procedure

    (iv) repealed statutes

(c) State statutes (alphabetically by state)

    (i) in current codification

    (ii) currently in force, but not in current codification (most recent first)

    (iii) rules of evidence and procedure

    (iv) repealed statutes (most recent first)

(d) Foreign statutes (alphabetically by jurisdiction)

    (i) currently in force

    (ii) repealed

(e) Municipal ordinances, etc.

Note: Although statutes usually follow cases in a multiple citation, an exception is made when a statute and a case construing it are cited. Where a case construes a statute the two citations should be separated by *"construed in":* Ind. Code § 475 (Burns' Ann. 1934), *construed in Hoffman v. State,* 75 Ind. 918, 38 N.E.2d 475 (1945).

(3) *Secondary Materials.* Within each of the following categories, citations are listed alphabetically by author or, if the author is unknown, by title.

(a) Books

(b) Articles

(c) Student written law review material (listed alphabetically by periodical)

(d) signed book reviews

(e) student-written book notes

(f) newspapers

(g) annotations

(h) unpublished materials

3. PARENTHETICALS INDICATING WEIGHT AND EXPLANATION

a. Parentheticals Indicating Weight. When a case is cited for material other than a clear non-alternative majority holding, indicate this in parentheses after the date of the case. Thus, (1) dicta, (2) concurring or dissenting opinions, (3) points decided by implication, (4) plurality opinions, and (5) points on which the holding of the court is not clear must be so indicated.

(1) *Dicta.* If the proposition was not necessary to the decision in that case, it is dictum; this fact must be conveyed. This information is shown by proceeding as follows:

(a) Place the word "dictum" in parentheses at the end of the citation.

(b) List the page on which the dictum appears in both the official and unofficial reporter, as well as the page on which the case begins. *Frederick v. Schwarz,* 10 Ohio St. 21, 23, 15 N.E. 359, 360 (1890) (dictum). Note, however, that if the dictum appears on the first page of the case in one of the reporters cited, it is unnecessary to repeat this page number in the citation. *Brag v. Snort,* 112 Va. 542, 543, 158 S.E. 615 (1929) (dictum).

(2) *Concurring or Dissenting Opinions.* If a dissenting or concurring opinion is cited, indicate that fact in parentheses at the end of the citation. *McLaughlin v. Walter,* 250 Pa. 206, 218, 195 A. 417, 425 (1915) (concurring opinion). To name the judge, cite: *See* Mr. Justice Black, dissenting in *Harkness v. Cass,* 315 U.S. 419, 480 (1939); or *Harkness v. Cass,* 315 U.S. 419, 480 (1939) (Black, J., dissenting).

(3) *Points Decided by Implication; Alternative Holdings.* Where the point for which the case is cited is obtained by implication, or where there is an alternative basis of decision, such should be indicated parenthetically. *Shayne v. David,* 21 U.S. (8 Wheat.) 22 (1823) (by implication); *Hobart v. Parson,* 20 Ohio St. 34 (1873) (alternative holding).

(4) *Plurality Opinions.* If an opinion was joined by only a plurality of judges, indicate the fact parenthetically. *Frontiero v. Richardson,* 411 U.S. 677 (1973) (plurality opinion).

(5) *Points with Holding Unclear:* If the holding of a case is not clear, indicate this fact by "holding unclear" in parentheses at the end of the citation. *Sacks v. Hart,* 325 U.S. 1 (1945) (holding unclear).

b. Explanatory Parentheticals.

(1) *Name of Judge Writing Opinion.* The name of the judge who wrote the opinion and other information relevant to the weight of the authority cited may be given in parentheses. *Ewing v. Ames,* 115 F.2d 25 (2d Cir. 1952) (L. Hand, J.).

(2) *Statement of Facts.* A brief statement of the facts or a comment on the case which helps explain the citation may also be enclosed in parentheses. *Greeley v. Jones,* 10 Hawaii 16 (1959) (joint tortfeasors); *Begley v. Louis,* 18 Vt. 127 (1864) (common law rule).

c. Order of Parentheticals. Parentheticals indicating weight should precede those giving other information. *Briffaut v. Gelston,* 219 Mass. 14, 191 N.E. 12 (1923) (by implication) (per curiam) ($10,000 verdict not excessive).

D. CITATION OF CASES

1. GENERAL RULES OF FORM

a. Parts of the Citation (Order and Form). Parts of a citation are given in the following order and form:

(1) *Case Name.* Names of both parties and the "v." between them are underlined (the equivalent of italics) and followed by a comma. *Langevoort v. Sidorov,* 422 U.S. 483 (1976). The parties' names can be shortened for the purpose of citation. Rules providing for such shortening are listed in subsections b and c of this part. In citing administrative decisions, use the full name of the first named party.

(2) *Reporter.* This part of the citation gives (a) the volume number, (b) the name of the reporter, and (c) the page number in the reporter on which the decision begins.

Abbreviations of the names of the reporters to be used may be found below in Parts D.2. and D.3.

If the reporter name is not sufficient to indicate which court made the decision, the court must be indicated in parentheses with the date at the end of the citation. *McDonald v. Cooper,* 254 Misc. 498, 50 N.Y.S.2d 891 (Sup.Ct. 1959).

(3) *Date.* The year is enclosed in parentheses at the end of the citation.

(4) *Subsequent and Prior History.* The prior and subsequent history of a case may be a necessary part of the citation. The subsections below explain when such history is

required. The history is explained by underlined explanatory words between the citations.

(a) Subsequent History. The subsequent history of a case is always given whenever the case is cited in full, with the exceptions that the history on remand and any denial of rehearing are omitted unless relevant for that which the case is cited. Note the use of commas. *Abrams v. Cushing,* 101 Mass. 362, 48 N.E. 384 (1901), *aff'd,* 200 U.S. 201 (1904); *Simkowitz v. Wyse,* 120 Pa. 381, 43 N.E. 760 (1911), *cert. denied,* 98 U.S. 859 (1912); *Donald J. Dietrich,* 39 T.C. 271 (1962), *rev'd,* 330 F.2d 985 (6th Cir. 1964).

(b) Prior History. The prior history of a case is given only if significant to the point for which the case is cited.

(c) Use of *"sub nom."* This phrase is used if the names of the parties differ on appeal. It is not used when the names of the parties are simply reversed. *Griswold v. Hall,* 282 F.2d 600 (1st Cir. 1960), *rev'd per curiam sub nom. Toepfer v. Hall,* 370 U.S. 400 (1962). Note that there is no comma after *"nom." Sub nom.* is used only with subsequent, not prior history.

b. Omissions in Case Names.

(1) *Secondary Parties.* Names of all parties (except the first listed on each side) and words (such as *et al.*) which indicate multiple parties are omitted. However, no portion of a partnership name may be omitted.

(2) *Procedural Phrases. Ex parte, In re,* and other procedural phrases can be omitted only in administrative actions and when adversary parties are named. *Ex rel.,* however, is retained even when adversary parties are named.

(3) *Given Names and Initials.* Those names of individuals are omitted in all but administrative actions, but names of business firms must always be given in full.

(4) *State Names.* "State of," "Commonwealth of," and "People of" are omitted except in citing decisions of that state, in which case only "People", "Commonwealth", or "State" should be retained. *Wolf v. Colorado,* 325 U.S. 25 (1949); *State v. Lehman,* 218 Miss. 412, 96 So. 2d 130 (1957); not *State of Mississippi v. Lehman.*

(5) *Phrases of location.* Phrases of location (such as ". . . of Boston") are omitted unless this leaves only one word in the name of a party or corporation or is the designa-

tion of a national or larger geographical area. Note: "of America" is always omitted after "United States."

(6) *Consolidated Actions.* If a case is the consolidation of two or more actions, cite only the first listed.

c. **Abbreviations in Case Names.**

(1) *Commonly abbreviated full names.* When the entire name of a party is commonly abbreviated to widely recognized initials, this may be done in the citation.

(2) *Abbreviations of words within names.* A word which is commonly abbreviated may be shortened in a citation if it is not the first word of the name of a party. Some words in this category are: Commissioner (Comm'r); Company (Co.); Consolidated (Consol.); Corporation (Corp.); Department (Dep't); Electric (Elec.); Insurance (Ins.); Mutual (Mut.); National (Nat'l); Society (Soc'y).

(3) *Railroads.* In giving railroad names, the first word is generally given in full, and the others abbreviated to the initial letter unless the name is very short or there is a recognized abbreviation for it or the words complete the name of a state, city or geographical entity begun by the first word. "Co." is never included. "R.R." or "Ry." is used as the abbreviation of "Railroad Company" or "Railway Company." *Baltimore & O.R.R. v. United States ex rel. Minneapolis, St. P. & Ste. M. Ry.; Lehigh Valley R.R. v. New York Cent. R.R.*

2. CITATIONS TO REPORTERS OF FEDERAL CASES

a. **Supreme Court of the United States.**

(1) *If the official report has appeared.* Citation to the official United States Reporter is sufficient for Supreme Court cases. *Jones v. Jones,* 206 U.S. 356 (1935). When citing any of the first 90 volumes of this reporter, indicate both the number of the volume as renumbered and the name of the report editor. *Green v. Biddle,* 21 U.S. (8 Wheat.) 16 (1823). Beginning with 91 U.S. (1875) the named reporter is disregarded and cases are cited simply as "U.S." The names of the cited report editors follow in the chronological order of their reports:

Dallas (cited: Dall.) (4 vol.) (1–4 U.S.)

Cranch (cited: Cranch) (9 vol.) (5–13 U.S.)

Wheaton (cited: Wheat.) (12 vol.) (14–25 U.S.)

Peters (cited: Pet.) (16 vol.) (26–41 U.S.)

Howard (cited: How.) (24 vol.) (42–65 U.S.)

Black (cited: Black) (2 vol.) (66–67 U.S.)

Wallace (cited: Wall.) (23 vol.) (68–90 U.S.)

(2) *If the official report has not appeared.* If the official report has not yet appeared, cite to Supreme Court Reporter (cited: S. Ct.), or, if not therein, to the United States Law Week (cited: U.S.L.W.). In the latter case, indicate the date of the decision, and the court. *Chandler v. Wilson,* 23 U.S. L.W. 406 (U.S. Nov. 8, 1954).

b. Lower Federal Courts.

(1) *Federal Reporter and Federal Reporter, Second Series* (since 1880) (Cited: F. and F.2d). These unofficial reporters have achieved approximately official status through constant use in the absence of an official reporter.

The court from which the decision came must be specially noted in parentheses since F. and F.2d cover a multitude of courts. The following courts are covered:

(a) Courts of Appeals. There are thirteen of these, one for each of the eleven regional circuits, one for the District of Columbia and one for the Federal Circuit. The number of the circuit must be included in the citation. *Jones v. Jones,* 173 F.2d 25 (1st Cir. 1949); *Mills v. Wilber,* 280 F. 25 (D.C. Cir. 1919).

(b) Circuit Courts (abolished 1912). *Cahoon v. Sand,* 180 F. 35 (C.C.S.D.N.Y. 1911).

(c) District Courts. There is at least one district court for each of the 50 states. In citing, name the district but not any division within it. Proper citation for United States District Court for the Eastern District of Illinois, Western Division, would be: *Jones v. Jones,* 180 F. 35 (E.D. Ill. 1901).

(d) Court of Customs and Patent Appeals. This should be cited to the official reporter only in the absence of the federal reporter. *Jones v. Jones,* 98 F.2d 73 (C.C. P.A. 1936).

(e) Court of Claims. This should be cited to the official reporter only in the absence of the federal reporter. *Gardiner v. Lyons,* 98 F.2d 73 (Ct.Cl. 1936).

(2) *Federal Supplement (since 1932) (cited:* F. Supp.). This includes decisions of the District Courts and of the Court of Claims (see above under Federal Reporter). *Cohen v. Hassett,* 192 F. Supp. 841 (S.D.N.Y. 1965); *Klein v. Gilbert,* 330 F. Supp. 210 (D.R.I. 1970).

(3) *Federal Rules Decisions (since 1938) (cited:* F.R.D.). This work includes decisions of all federal courts interpreting and applying the Federal Rules of Criminal and Civil Procedure. If the same case is printed in both F.R.D. and F. Supp. or F.2d cite to the latter only. The court must be indicated if the sole cite is to F.R.D.

(4) *Federal Cases.* Federal Cases contains many of the federal court cases decided prior to 1880. The decisions in the thirty volumes are arranged alphabetically and not chronologically, each case being numbered. Proper citation is: *Jones v. Smith,* 14 F. Cas. 452 (No. 7312) (C.C.S.D.N.J. 1870).

(5) *The Circuit Court of Appeals Reports (cited:* C.C.A.). These are now discontinued and because their materials since 1880 are also included in the Federal Reporter, citation to this special series should not be used unless the case is not reported in the National Reporter System or in Federal Cases.

(6) *American Law Reports, Annotated (cited:* A.L.R., A.L.R.2d, A.L.R.3d) (1919—to date). American Law Reports contains selected state and federal cases, some of which are extensively annotated.

c. **Administrative Bodies.** Cite only to the official report if the case appears therein. Use only the full name of the first named party in citing reports of administrative bodies. *Ernest J. Brown,* 27 B.T.A. 660 (1932). If the official report has not yet been bound and paginated, cite by case number and full date. *Mario v. Carpaty,* 29 T.C. No. 12 (Dec. 22, 1968).

d. **Incomplete Citations.**

(1) *Where there is no official citation.* If for any reason a case does not appear or has not yet appeared in the official reports, cite only the unofficial reporter. *Jones v. Jones,* 256 S. Ct. 209 (1969); *Keeton v. O'Connell,* 218 So. 2d 842 (Fla. 1968).

(2) *Where the case has not yet appeared in any report.* The full texts of United States Supreme Court and other federal court opinions can generally be found very soon after they are rendered in the United States Law Week, which should be cited if it is the only available reference. *Jones v. Mullaney,* 26 U.S.L.W. 4416 (U.S. Jan. 7, 1959). If the opinion does not appear in any report, then the following form may be used: *Jones v. Jones,* Civil No. 51–1250 (D.Mass., filed Mar. 1, 1959).

3. CITATIONS TO REPORTERS OF STATE CASES

State court cases should be cited to both the official reporter and one unofficial reporter. Cases reported with independent pagination in two reports of the National Reporter System (New York Court of Appeals cases since 1 N.Y.2d 1 and California Supreme Court cases since 53 Cal.2d 187) should be cited to the official and both West reporters. *Stimley v. Starzel,* 114 N.H. 84, 176 N.E.2d 155 (1957); *Hassett v. Wood,* 2 N.Y.2d 727, 138 N.E.2d 729, 157 N.Y.S.2d 364 (1956); *Schuldofer v. Dodge,* 60 Cal. 2d 208, 359 P.2d 35, 50 Cal. Rptr. 47 (1960).

a. Official Reporters.

(1) *Abbreviation of state names.* The names of all states and territories (except Alaska, Hawaii, Idaho, Iowa, Ohio and Utah) are abbreviated in citations as follows: Ala., Ariz., Ark., Cal., C.Z., Colo., Conn., Del., D.C., Fla., Ga., Ill., Ind., Kan., Ky., La., Me., Md., Mass., Mich., Minn., Miss., Mo., Mont., Neb., Nev., N.H., N.J., N.M., N.Y., N.C., N.D., Okla., Or., Pa., P.R., R.I., S.C., S.D., Tenn., Tex., Vt., V.I., Va., Wash., W.Va., Wis., Wyo.

(2) *Early state reports.* The early state reports were prepared by and listed under the names of individual reporters. Proper abbreviations of these early reports may be found in the appendix of *Black's Law Dictionary.* The abbreviations for the more commonly cited early reports appear in *A Uniform System of Citation* (13th ed. 1981). Where the jurisdiction is not shown by such a citation, it should appear in the parentheses with the date. *Jones v. Doe,* 4 Wend. 10 (N.Y. 1835). *Roe v. Smith,* 5 Wend. 13, 12 Am. Dec. 68 (N.Y. 1836).

(3) *Exceptional state reports.* In most jurisdictions the official reporter covers only the decisions of the highest appellate court in the state. The court need not be specifically named where this is the case, since the information as to the court is conveyed by the name of the report itself. In other jurisdictions there are several courts reported in a single reporter. In this latter situation, it is always necessary to indicate the particular court from which the decision came unless the court is the highest in the state. If the court is clear from the name of the reporter the court of decision need not be indicated even if it is not the highest in the state. *Morris v. Benbassat,* 210 P.2d 887 (Okla. 1955); *Fried v. Adler,* 28 App. Div. 2d 73, 14 N.Y.S.2d 449 (1951). A list of official state reporters which cover more than one court and official reporters cited other than merely by name

of the state alone can be found in *A Uniform System of Citation* (13th ed. 1981).

b. Unofficial Reporters.

(1) *National Reporter System (West).* This is the most desirable of all unofficial reporters to cite, but the first of the West series began in 1879. The West Company puts out the regional reporters covering state court cases, with most now appearing in the second series for the region. The proper citation and citation spacing for each sectional reporter is given below.

Reporter	1st Series	2d Series
Atlantic	A.	A.2d
California	Cal. Rptr.	
New York Supplement	N.Y.S.	N.Y.S.2d
North Eastern	N.E.	N.E.2d
North Western	N.W.	N.W.2d
Pacific	P.	P.2d
Southern	So.	So. 2d
South Eastern	S.E.	S.E.2d
South Western	S.W.	S.W.2d

(2) *Annotated Reports System.* The reporters within this system are as selective as the West System is complete. However, for cases prior to 1879, these will provide an unofficial reporter citation. Since 1888, the major emphasis has been upon printing cases of widespread interest and including an annotation. See the section on citing secondary authority for the form of citing the annotation alone. Citation should include parenthetical indication of court and jurisdiction.

American Law Reports Annotated (A.L.R.; A.L.R.2d; A.L.R.3d)

Lawyers' Reports Annotated (Note: This series had two further series, the second being called "New Series" and the third being called "Dated Series." The following illustrates the correct citation form, with the date of 1915 being illustrative for the "Dated Series": L.R.A.; L.R.A. (n.s.); 1915 L.R.A.).

American Annotated Cases (Am. Ann. Cas.)

American and English Annotated Cases (Am. & Eng. Ann. Cas.)

American State Reports (Am. St. R.)

American Reports (Am. R.)

American Decisions (Am. Dec.)

c. Incomplete Citations.

(1) *Where there is no official citation.* Sometimes a case will appear in an unofficial and not in the official reports, particularly if it is from a lower state court. Cite the unofficial reporter, including the jurisdiction or court in the parentheses before the date. *Jones v. Jones,* 176 N.E. 28 (Ill. 1965). *Jones v. Jones,* 137 N.Y.S. 25 (Sup. Ct. 1925).

(2) *Where the case has not yet appeared in any report.* Cite by docket number, court and full date. *Black v. White,* Civil No. 51–1250 (Pa. Super. Ct. May 1, 1959).

E. CITATION OF STATUTES AND CONSTITUTIONS

1. IN GENERAL

a. Session Laws and Compilations. Statute reports may roughly be divided into two classes, session laws and compilations. The session laws are usually printed in the chronological order of enactment and are nearly always official reports of the legislature; compilations are usually arranged according to subject matter and may or may not have official status. Because of the large variety of titles which are employed, it is impossible to give a list of both classes for each state and their proper method of citation.

(1) *Compilations.* Cite a state statute only to the latest official statutory compilation, if it appears therein. The official compilations are not always up to date, and they may not include all of the statutes. In the latter event, cite the statute to the unofficial compilation. Ill. Rev. Stat. ch. 111½, §§ 35.27–.31 (1963); Mass. Gen. Laws Ann. ch. 94, § 19 (1954); Tenn. Code Ann. § 8582 (1955).

(2) *Session Laws.* If the statute is contained in neither official nor unofficial compilations, cite it to the session laws. 1975 N.Y. Laws.

b. General Rules on Form. In contrast to cases, statutes are not underlined or italicized. Statutes are primary authorities and should be listed as such in the Table of Citations. A listing of the statutes cited should precede a listing of the secondary authorities used.

2. FEDERAL STATUTES

a.   General Form of Citation. In citing United States statutes that are in those parts of the United States Code which have been enacted into positive law, indicate only the title, section and date of the code along with the name of the statute if it has one. Declaratory Judgment Act, 28 U.S.C. §§ 2201–02 (1959).   The titles of U.S.C. which have been enacted into positive law as of 1982 are titles 1, 3–5, 9–11, 13, 14, 17, 18, 23, 28, 31, 32, 35, 37–39, 44 and 49.

For all other titles the language of United States Statutes at Large (cited: Stat.) is authoritative.   Both United States Code and United States Code Annotated (cited: U.S.C.A.) cross-reference code sections to U.S. Statutes at Large.   U.S. Statutes at Large need not be cited unless the language in the U.S. Statutes at Large differs materially from that in United States Code. Clayton Act, 15 U.S.C. § 16 (1959);   Federal Trade Commission Act, 38 Stat. 747 (1914), 15 U.S.C. § 78 (1959).

b.   Amended Statutes. It may be relevant that the statutory language being cited differs from an earlier or later version of the statute.   The following rules indicate how this information, if desired, may be conveyed in the citation.

(1) When a section is amended so that the subsequent version completely supersedes and repeals the earlier version, the version now in force is cited to the code and the version no longer in force is cited to the session laws.   If discussing the former version, cite: Clayton Act sec. 7, ch. 25, sec. 7, 38 Stat. 730 (1914), *amended by* 15 U.S.C. sec. 18 (1964).   If discussing the present version, cite: Clayton Act sec. 7, 15 U.S.C. § 18 (1964), *formerly* ch. 25, sec. 7, 38 Stat. 730 (1914).

(2) When a statutory section is amended so that the subsequent version only makes additions to and does not repeal the former, cite both versions to the code.   In discussing the present version, cite: 28 U.S.C. § 2201(b) (Supp. I 1965), *amending* 28 U.S.C. § 2201 (1964).   If discussing the former version, cite: 28 U.S.C. § 2201 (1964), *as amended,* 28 U.S.C. § 2201(b) (Supp. I 1965).

c.   New Statutes. Statutes enacted since the last complete United States Code should be cited by the most recent U.S.C. Supplement.   United States Mandamus Act, 28 U.S.C. § 83 (Supp. V 1964).

Statutes enacted subsequent to the last U.S.C. Supplement should be cited by U.S.C.A. pocket supplements.   18 U.S.C.A. § 14 (Supp.1965).

d. Statutes No Longer in Force and Statutes Not Appearing in Any Edition of United States Code. These are cited by reference only to the Statutes at Large (cited: Stat.). Give the chapter number and the name or the full date if there is no name. The fact that the act is no longer in force as cited must be indicated parenthetically. Act of Sept. 8, 1950, ch. 924, § 2, 64 Stat. 798 (repealed 1955). Since the 85th Congress, the public law number should be used in place of the chapter number.

e. Statutes Enacted by the Current Legislature. These are cited: Pub. L. No. 94–32, § 20(a) (June 11, 1975). "94–" means "94th Congress."

f. Internal Revenue Code. When dealing with federal tax questions, cite the Internal Revenue Code of 1954, if the section cited is in force at the time of writing. I.R.C. § 301 (1984). Sections of the Internal Revenue Code of 1939 must be cited to Int. Rev. Code of 1939, ch. 1, § 115(d), 53 Stat. 47 (now I.R.C. § 301). Revenue Acts prior to 1939 are cited by name and to Stat. Revenue Act of 1924, ch. 234, § 200, 43 Stat. 454.

g. Rules of Procedure. The Federal Rules of Civil and Criminal Procedure may conveniently be cited as statutes. Fed. R. Civ. P. 19(b); Fed. R. Crim. P. 42(b).

3. STATE STATUTES

a. Official Compilation. Cite state statutes to the latest official compilation; if not contained there, cite the statute to the preferred unofficial compilation. Ill. Rev. Stat. ch. 32, § 439.50 (1963); Mass. Gen. Laws ch. 41, § 95 (1932); N.J. Rev. Stat. § 43:22–5 (Supp. 1955).

b. Unofficial Compilation. If the statute has been amended or enacted subsequent to the most recent supplement to the official compilation, cite the preferred unofficial compilation. Pa. Stat. Ann. tit. 2, § 4656.13 (1959).

c. New York and California Codes. The New York and California Codes are cited by the name of the particular law or code with indication of date and edition. Cal. Agric. Code § 351 (West 1954); N.Y. Banking Law § 121 (McKinney 1964).

d. Uniform Acts. Uniform acts cited as the law of a particular state should be cited to the state statute in the manner described above. When citing a uniform act as such (that is, when not citing it as the law of any particular state), there is no requirement that the date of promulgation be given, unless the act has been withdrawn. Uniform Warehouse Receipts Act § 40 (withdrawn 1906). The Uniform Commercial Code is cited in abbreviated form. U.C.C. § 2–505.

4. ENGLISH STATUTES

Cite the name, year of sovereign's reign, chapter, and section.

Statute of Gloucester, 1278, 6 Edw. 1, c. 8, § 1; Copyright Act, 1911, 1 & 2 Geo. V, c. 46, § 2. Where the statute has no name or where the name does not include the date, put the date in parentheses at the end. After 1962, regnal years are omitted.

5. CONSTITUTIONS

Constitutions should precede statutes in any listing (for instance, in the Table of Citations section of the brief), but are cited under the general heading of statutes. U.S. Const. art. III, § 8; U.S. Const. amend. XIV, § 2; Mont. Const. art. 8, § 16.

The date is given only where a constitution other than the one in force is cited. Ga. Const. art. II, § 1 (1875).

F. CITATION TO SECONDARY AUTHORITY

1. AMERICAN LAW INSTITUTE RESTATEMENTS

Publications of the American Law Institute should be cited as follows:

Restatement of Torts § 90 (1936).

Restatement (Second) of Conflict of Laws § 20 (1958).

Restatement of Trusts § 9, comment *b* (1935).

Restatement of Contracts § 106 (Tent. Draft No. 1, 1929).

Restatement of Agency Neb. Annot. § 5 (1934).

7 *A.L.I. Proceedings* 256 (1930).

2. TREATISES

Citations to treatises should follow these rules.

a. Name of author. The name is cited with the last name and first initial, unless more would aid identification. W. Prosser.

b. Title of book (underlined or italicised).

c. Page or section number.

d. Edition and year (in parentheses).

e. The volume number of a multiple volume work precedes the name of the author. The following are examples of single and multiple volume works: R. Brooks & W. Warren, *Understanding Poetry* 524 (1938); 2 F. Wharton, *Criminal Law and Procedure* § 572 (12th ed. 1957).

f. There is no comma between the title and the section or page number.

g.   The page or section number may be omitted in the Table of Citations, particularly if many sections are cited.

h.   Always cite to the most recent edition of a work which gives the matter in question.   1 S. Williston, *Sales* § 72 (rev. ed. 1948).

i.   In special cases treatises are identified by the editor: 5 *American Law of Property* § 22.15 (A.J. Casner ed. 1952).

j.   In a few time-honored works the edition is left out and the star page, the page of the original printing, is referred to.   2 W. Blackstone, *Commentaries* * 152.   E. Coke, *Littleton* * 5.

3. LAW REVIEW ARTICLES AND NOTES

Abbreviations of the names of law reviews are listed in *A Uniform System of Citation* (13th ed. 1981).   Note that California is abbreviated to Calif.; Columbia, to Colum.; and that Texas is not abbreviated.

a.   Leading Articles.   Citations of leading articles should give the following information in the following order:

(1) Author (last name only), followed by a comma.

(2) Title of article (underlined), followed by a comma.

(3) Volume of law review.   If the periodical has no volume number, use the year of publication.   67 Harv. L. Rev. 710 (1955); 1938 Wis. L. Rev. 307.

(4) Name of review.

(5) Page number on which article begins.   Exception: if the article appears in two or more parts, cite the page number upon which each part begins.   But when citing to specific material within one part, give only the first page of that part and the page upon which the material appears.   Fuller, *Legal Fictions*, 25 Ill. L. Rev. 363, 513, 865 (1930–31).

(6) Date (in parentheses).

b.   **Law Review Notes and Comments.**   Student material, other than short commentaries, is cited by the designation used in the publishing review.   The name of a student author is never given, but the title is always included.   Note, *Speluncean Explorers*, 45 Colum. L. Rev. 382 (1945); Comment, *Civil Rights Act*, 49 Mich. L. Rev. 261 (1950).

Short commentaries, such as Recent Decisions and Case Notes, are cited without identification.   8 U. Chi. L. Rev. 132 (1940).

Recent case write-ups are cited: 28 Colum. L. Rev. 130 (1928).   When these are used together with the case, cite: *Beale v. Williston*, 71 F.2d 334 (2d Cir. 1934), *noted in* 43 Yale L.J. 881. If the date of the write-up differs, give both dates: *Jones v.*

York, 310 Mass. 613, 8 N.E.2d 790 (1939), *noted in* 53 Harv. L. Rev. 806 (1940).

4. ANNOTATIONS

As a general rule, do not cite decisions to the A.L.R. or L.R.A. These materials may, however, be used for an additional unofficial citation where the cited case is reported therein and is the subject of an annotation. Indicate the page upon which the report, not the annotation, begins. When citing the annotation alone, indicate the page upon which the annotation begins, and the date of publication of the volume. Annot., 12 A.L.R.2d 382 (1950).

5. ADDITIONAL SOURCES

a. Encyclopedias. On very rare occasions, additional sources might include references to Corpus Juris, Corpus Juris Secundum, American Jurisprudence, American Jurisprudence 2d, and Ruling Case Law. These, in the order just given, are cited for the subject heading "Trial" as follows: 29 C.J. *Trial* § 24 (1944); 33 C.J.S. *Trial* § 21 (1955); 19 Am.Jur. *Trial* § 21 (1946); 6 Am.Jur.2d *Assignments* § 7 (1957); 19 R.C.L. *Trial* § 21 (1952).

b. Newspapers. In citing newspapers give the name of the paper, the full date, the section (if any), the page, and the column. N.Y. Times, Jan. 21, 1936, § 3, at 1, col. 4. A signed article (but not a news report) is cited by author and title.

c. Briefs. Citation of an opponent's brief or an earlier brief (*e.g.,* citation of appellant's brief in his own reply brief) in the same litigation need only identify the brief and page. Brief for Appellee at 10. If a brief in another lawsuit is cited, the case must be clearly identified. Brief for Appellant at 26, *Burka v. Cogan,* 248 F.2d 60 (D.C.Cir. 1974).

Chapter VI

ORAL ADVOCACY

After the long and often wearisome task of preparing a brief comes the culmination of an advocate's efforts—oral argument. Going into court and trying to persuade judges to find in your client's favor is a very different challenge from briefwriting, and learning to deliver an effective argument takes practice. It is not, however, an ordeal to be endured, as some first year law students believe. If you are thoroughly prepared, and confident enough to relax while you speak and answer questions, oral argument can actually be fun. Indeed, some consider oral argument "the most exhilarating and exciting task that the advocate is ever called upon to perform." [1]

Oral argument is a fixed part of the American tradition of advocacy. In the early years of the Supreme Court, arguments lasted for hours, if not days. In fact, the arguments of Daniel Webster and Luther Martin in *McCulloch v. Maryland* lasted six days.[2] While the amount of time available to advocates today for oral argument has been dramatically reduced, it nonetheless presents a valuable opportunity to convince the court of the merits of the case and to dispel any lingering doubts a particular judge may have.

The basic structure of an appellate oral argument is simple and direct. The appellant rises first to give a short introduction to the nature and facts of the case, and then to explain why the court should reverse the lower tribunal's decision. The appellee then presents his side of the case. Finally, the appellant has an opportunity to rebut her opponent's assertions. Throughout the argument the judges are likely to interrupt counsels' presentations with questions. By listening carefully to the judges' questions, the advocates can discover how a judge perceives the case and immediately respond to those perceptions. The process is dynamic and complex, and many have said that it is an art truly mastered by only a few appellate lawyers.

As in briefwriting, there are many styles and approaches to oral argument: for example, flamboyant, subdued, aggressive, or deferential. There is no "right" way to prepare for and present an argument. However, your personality, the strengths and weaknesses of your case, and the peculiar characteristics of your audience will certainly be among the factors that will shape your oral argument.

[1] J. Kaufman, "Appellate Advocacy in the Federal Courts," 79 F.R.D. 165, 170 (1977).

[2] J.W. Davis, "The Argument of an Appeal," 26 A.B.A.J. 895, 896 (1940).

124

This chapter presents more clearly the options available to you in choosing the most appropriate style of oral argument for you.

A. PREPARING FOR ORAL ARGUMENT

Preparation is actually a two-step process: study and rehearsal. To be truly ready to stand before a judge and argue your case, you must know your arguments and the authorities they rest on inside and out. Spending sufficient time rereading cases and mastering their facts is essential. This enables you to distinguish adverse precedent without hesitation and to feel confident answering the judges' inevitable questions. You need to rehearse, whether in front of a friend, a mirror, or a tape recorder, to become comfortable expressing your arguments orally.

While both kinds of preparation are important, students sometimes spend so much time rehearsing that they sacrifice mastering their case. Overrehearsal may make the final argument somewhat stale and lacking in sincerity. In addition, an overrehearsed oralist may "lock into" positions prior to her appearance before the court and lose the flexibility necessary to meet the other side's arguments.

What follows is a step-by-step outline of the basic techniques for preparing for oral argument.

1. Study the Record and Authorities. Success in any aspect of oral argument requires complete mastery of the record and briefs before the court. There is no shortcut here. The record and briefs are the basic documents for informing and convincing the court and your job is to know their contents thoroughly. Because the court's decision ultimately turns on the facts, you must have an intimate knowledge of the events giving rise to the cause of action and issues and facts cited in the lower court's opinion. Your ability to answer the court's questions with an apt reference to the record will enhance the court's confidence in other aspects of your presentation.[3]

You cannot gain an understanding of the record or of the particular facts of cases you cite by relying solely upon your brief or knowledge gained in the process of brief preparation. Oral argument is a separate part of advocacy that requires independent preparation. Indeed, arguments that are not amenable to written presentation may be raised orally before the court (although court rules may restrict the use of cases not cited in the brief), and you may move to correct what judges perceive as flaws in your brief.

Ideally, you should have a complete understanding of all the cases cited in both sides' briefs. Studying the cases and determining how to analogize from helpful ones and distinguish harmful ones are critically important. You may want to spend longer on cases the

---

[3] Davis, 26 A.B.A.J. at 896.

court is likely to feel are decisive and those upon which interpretive disagreements exist, particularly if you are pressed for time. Note that moot court judges are likely to raise questions about particular cases. To aid in study, retention, and referencing facts and authorities, you may want to write up short case abstracts and index the record. However, you should become so familiar with the record and relevant cases that you can discuss them without referring to notes.

2. Analyze the Arguments. To devise strategy and choose the arguments to make orally, you need to understand all the issues and arguments arising from the case. Make a methodical attempt to break down the arguments presented in your own and your opponent's briefs. This dissection, along with knowledge of the record and authorities, will give you a complete background against which to make strategic and tactical choices concerning both substance and style.

a. Using your core theory. Long before the argument stage, the advocate develops her "core theory," the one or two sentence explanation of the essence of her case. (Recall the discussion of the core theory in Chapter II, Reading the Record.) The advocate will build her case on this basic framework, embellishing the central theory to respond to judge's concerns and explain fully why the court should rule in her client's favor. Because oral argument focuses attention on the most compelling aspects of a case, you may simplify and improve your presentation by choosing arguments that tightly revolve around your case's core theory. In many instances, a powerful case stresses basically one idea, without directly stating that notion over and over, but by coming at that idea from different angles—facts, laws, policy. In organizing your argument, keep in mind the relationship between a particular assertion and the core theory, and decide whether that relationship can be simply and succinctly conveyed orally.

b. Understanding specific arguments. Understand the specific arguments made in the briefs, for they will occupy most of your actual arguing time. In asserting and attacking these arguments, you will be asked to blend issues with facts and law. Remember that just as in writing the brief, you must argue the facts of your case and explain why existing legal rules should or should not apply.

(1) *Ranking the Arguments' Importance.* As you develop your understanding of the arguments, you should begin to make judgments about the merits of particular points. First, rank arguments in terms of importance to the results desired. Because you have only a short period of time in which to argue, you need to decide which arguments are worth emphasizing. There is no single method for making this difficult decision, but some factors to weigh are whether a written argument is too complex to make effectively orally; what

policy considerations may move a judge to rule your way; which argument is your "weakest link" and thus likely to be the court's focal concern; which argument is most powerful or convincing; and whether you are arguing with or against current trends in the law. In addition, you must know exactly what the lower court did and exactly what you seek to have affirmed or reversed. Indeed, one favorite question of moot court judges is simply, "Counsel, what is it that you want me to do here?"

(2) *Evaluating the Arguments' Merits.* You should also identify the strengths and weaknesses of the arguments. Be objective when making this judgment: look to the merits of your opponent's arguments even if they were presented poorly. The court will probably confront you with the essence of your opponent's arguments; in many cases the court will present your opponent's positions better than your opponent does. Be objective about your own arguments as well. The judges will be most likely to object to those points that are the most innovative or lacking in significant case authority. Every argument has a weak point; make sure you are prepared to respond to an attack on your arguments' frailties.

3. Strategy and Style. Oral argument is akin to a dramatic performance. Just as the actor must rehearse many times before the curtain rises or the camera rolls, so too the advocate must master the record and practice delivering her argument. A good actor would also think through a character's motivations, responses and actions in order to flesh out the role and improve his portrayal. Similarly, the advocate must step back from the details of the case and consider the strategic and stylistic choices she must make. Unless the advocate has a clear idea of what she wants oral argument to accomplish and how she will feel most comfortable at the podium, most of the "nuts and bolts" preparation discussed elsewhere may be wasted.

The strategy and style of an oral argument will probably be related to the strategy and style of the brief, but they differ to the extent that the goals of oral argument differ. While the brief lays out your arguments and supports them with reference to legal authority, oral argument gives you the chance to present those arguments to a panel of judges and to try to persuade them by answering their questions smoothly and sensibly. Oral argument provides you with the opportunity to emphasize your strongest points and create a lasting—and winning—impression on the court. Moreover, if your brief contains a complex, innovative argument, the oral argument is your only chance to clarify that section of your brief so that it can have the fullest impact possible.

How you choose to structure your argument depends on a number of factors. The nature of your client's case is important. For example, representing a paraplegic victim of an automobile accident against the allegedly drunken driver of the other car calls for a different tone than representing an investor who claims to have been defrauded by a company's failure to disclose contingent liability in its annual financial statements.

Similarly, whether your client is appellant or appellee will have great bearing. Appellant speaks first and has the opportunity to choose to raise particular issues and to set the tone of the argument. The appellee, on the other hand, can tailor his argument to the concerns of the court evident in their questions to appellant. The opportunity for rebuttal gives appellant the last word, but in another sense appellee has the upper hand since appellant seeks to overturn a lower court judgment already entered against him.

Finally, your choice should be informed by institutional factors, including whether your case is in state or federal court, what arguments are likely to appeal to particular judges based on their ideological predilections, and whether the bench is "hot" or "cold"—that is, whether the judges are likely to have read your brief or at least have a glancing familiarity with the case before you open your mouth.

The strategic choices you make will dominate your decisions on presenting your argument, dealing with questions, handling precedent, and choosing which arguments to make and how to make them. As you plan for your own day in court and develop your own style, remember that there is no formula for the perfect oral argument. Each case is different and requires fresh thought, analysis, judgments, and preparation. Remember too that no advocate wins all the time, although every good advocate tries to.

4. Prepare Arguments for Oral Presentation. Once you have considered strategic issues and have evaluated the strengths, weaknesses, and relative importance of arguments, you are ready to begin organizing and preparing the arguments you intend to make in court.

Whatever arguments you decide to make, you will need to prepare written notes, even though you may never refer to them during the argument itself. As Justice Jackson once said, "Few lawyers are gifted with memory and composure to argue a case without papers of any kind before them. It is not necessary to try." [4] A court will not be impressed by an advocate who uses no notes, but a court will disapprove of an advocate who, once questioned, is unable to remember his argument. A few brief notes will help you avoid this pitfall.

Preparing written outlines or notes serves several functions. Sketching out your arguments may help you to focus and refine them, as well as to commit them to memory. However, abbreviated

[4] R. Jackson, "Advocacy Before the United States Supreme Court," 37 A.B. A.J. 801, 861 (1951).

outlines and catch phrases are probably more useful, since you will not be reading a finely honed script but will be engaged in conversation with the judges. Outlines allow the advocate to be sure that she covers the most essential points. In general, remember that the process of developing the outline is a far more important part of preparation than is the end product itself. Thinking, not writing, is the critical step, because judges are bound to ask you questions that will require you to think on your feet.

While notes of some kind are advisable, you should not and indeed must not write out a pat speech. In fact, the procedural rules for the federal appellate courts prohibit the reading of briefs.[5] Instead, make your notes short, with catch phrases that will allow you to recall at a glance the whole substance of an argument.

Some students decide to write out the first minute (about a page) of their argument. While reading this introduction may make the opening moments easier if you are not used to public speaking, it is nothing but a crutch that has to be discarded eventually. Write it out, if you must, but leave it behind when you move to the lectern so that you can begin your presentation with your eyes on the judges. By that time, if you have prepared sufficiently, you will be so familiar with your case that you can rely on your instincts to carry you through.

5. Anticipate Questions and Responses. In moot court competition, judges ask questions incessantly. For the novice advocate, developing the ability to answer questions presents the most formidable challenge. If you carefully anticipate questions and prepare answers, you will welcome the judges' inquiries. After all, your role in oral argument is to explain your position, and it will be easier to explain if a judge tells you exactly what troubles him about the case. A lively interchange between judge and advocate is what makes oral argument exhilarating. Time passes much more quickly when one is under fire, and the argument focuses more closely on the issues the judges deem relevant. The judges' questions transform the argument from a staid speech into a dynamic conversation.

From the very beginning of your preparation for oral argument you should be thinking about and jotting down a "question list." Put yourself in the judges' position as you read the record and the briefs. Try to pinpoint factual inconsistencies, expansive readings of the law, and barely distinguishable adverse cases, all of which are likely to arouse a judge's interest.

Prepare to answer questions just as you prepared the affirmative arguments. However, always maintain flexibility in developing an-

[5] Fed. R. App. P. 34(c).

swers since the judges' questions will inevitably differ somewhat from the ones for which you prepared.

Your ability to answer questions will depend on your understanding of the case and the arguments put forward by both sides. Anticipating questions and devising responses will allow you to move smoothly between answering a question to advancing the argument if the judges sit back and listen. The more times you are successful in that transition, the better your oral argument will be.

6. Rehearse Your Argument. Practicing your oral presentation is the most effective way to improve your argument, both substantively and stylistically. After all, as one writer asks, why "would any appellate counsel stand up in the appellate court and give that court a rough draft of his oral argument?" [6]

Rehearsal serves several functions. It allows you to practice emphasis, timing, pronunciation, and other delivery techniques, and to grow comfortable using the argument's particular vocabulary. It gives practice in handling questions, and often leads to the formulation of more questions or the substantive improvement of the argument. Finally, it allows you to be sure that the argument is complete, building confidence that will relieve the pressure when you are called to the lectern.

You should rehearse in live court situations where others can react to the argument and delivery and you can develop a sense of just how long it will take to cover every important point. (Many students are surprised to find that their limited time is up well before they have completed their argument.) A moot court team provides an excellent forum for rehearsal, allowing both the appellant and appellee halves of the team to challenge each other and to develop and practice arguments. The opportunity to confront the strongest opposing arguments in a practice oral argument will make the real argument more cohesive and polished.

Practicing alone before audio or video tape recorders may be less effective for some people, since it does not provide for listener response and may divert attention from the argument to the technology. However, reviewing your recorded performance gives you the chance to detect weaknesses in the argument, awkward phrases, hesitations, wordiness, flailing arms, and other flaws in delivery. If no friend or classmate is willing to listen to you rehearse and if recording equipment is unavailable, practice in front of a mirror or in the shower. In general, some rehearsal (even by yourself) is better than none at all.

[6] F. Hartnett, "Effective Oral Argument," 18 Prac. Law. 51, 59 (1972).

B. ORGANIZING THE ORAL ARGUMENT

1. Basic Structure of Oral Argument.[7] The decisions you make with regard to framing issues, choosing arguments, and setting the proper tone will probably be made within the context of a fixed structure for your presentation. This section discusses the various elements contained in a traditional oral presentation. You need not use this basic framework in your oral argument; indeed, the appellee's argument, in particular, may as a matter of strategy radically differ from the model. However, most oral presentations do conform, at least roughly, to this framework. As a general rule, you should change places in your imagination with the judges. You should ask yourself what a judge would like to know first about the case. What manner of presentation would immediately inform the judge of the central issue? What is an interesting, logical, respectful and positive approach? The traditional model is one commonsense approach to answering these questions.

a. The opening statement. The opening statement briefly and succinctly introduces counsel and describes the nature of the case. Counsel introduces himself in a formal yet simple way by giving his name and his relationship to his client. For example:

> May it please the court, my name is Robin Ball. I represent the appellants, Rebecca and Scott Bell-Wesley.

Your initial introduction of the case to the court should combine the necessary facts and legal analysis to describe the nature of the case and enable the judges to focus their experience and understanding on specific issues presented. State the question concisely and present it so as to include the fundamental contention sympathetically, but rationally.

An introduction that launches into a contorted description of procedural history or immediately begins reciting facts gives the court inadequate background for the arguments that follow. In either case, avoid a confusing opening like this:

> This case comes here on appeal to review a judgment of the Superior Court for the State of Ames which, after rejecting plaintiffs' legal claim, was entered for defendant.

> The facts involve an action by plaintiff for damages resulting from Dr. O'Toole's negligent performance of a vasectomy which led to the wrongful birth of plaintiffs' child.

Be sure to include all the information the court needs to understand your argument. An opening like this one plunges straight into the facts without letting the court know what questions it must resolve. The court will either lose interest or interrupt. Occasionally

---

[7] This section is based on Davis, 26 A.B.A.J. 895.

moot court judges are reduced to prying facts and issues out of students by a kind of cross-examination. This means that the student is neither doing his job nor helping his case.

In this situation, the presentation could have been very simple and clear:

> This case is here on appeal from the Superior Court of Ames. The Bell-Wesleys seek to establish that the defendant's negligent performance of a vasectomy creates an actionable wrongful birth claim. The Bell-Wesleys contend that as a result of Dr. O'Toole's negligence, they should recover damages for lost earnings, the costs of raising their son, Frank, pain and suffering, emotional trauma, and the sacrifice of their chosen lifestyle.

From such an introduction, the court knows at the outset what the questions are, and will listen to the facts with some appreciation of their relevance.

In team situations, the first speaker should introduce both himself and his teammate. The second speaker will repeat her own name before launching into her half of the argument. In addition, the first speaker should outline for the court the issues that each of the advocates will develop. For example:

> I will argue that wrongful birth is actionable as a standard medical malpractice claim. My co-counsel will demonstrate that the Bell-Wesleys are entitled to the types of damages just mentioned. The facts, as found by the Superior Court, are as follows . . ..

This simple device enables the court to organize its own questioning efficiently.

b. Statement of the facts. As in the brief, the oral statement of facts sets the stage for resolving legal issues in a specific factual setting. The court wants to know what the circumstances are behind this dispute or controversy, since the court's job is ultimately that of favoring one party over another. Delving into legal issues without telling the court the facts is asking the judge to decide an abstract question of legal principle rather than a specific controversy. Do not assume that the court knows any of the facts prior to the argument; state every critical fact. Time constraints and strategic choices should prompt you to eliminate all but the most relevant facts.

The statement of facts must be framed and delivered to present your point of view and the merits of your client's case. Remember, however, that if your statement of the facts is slanted or misleading, you will lose credibility with the court. A carefully organized statement of the facts can present the operative facts fairly and still compel the court to reach the desired conclusion.

Practice the statement of facts with someone unfamiliar with the case to see if you are clearly conveying the important information. Because the statement should be as short as possible and still achieve the desired goal, succinctness and precision are essential.

In team situations, only the first speaker for each side gives the statement of facts. It must highlight facts important to both partners' arguments, however. As for the appellee, a complete restatement of the facts is usually unnecessary. If appellee believes that appellant has omitted or mischaracterized particular facts, however, she should mention that to the court.

c. Concise outline of legal arguments. After presenting the facts that suggest the legal questions involved, a concise outline of the legal argument is in order. It is akin to the brief's table of contents, where the argument headings double as a summary outline of the entire argument. Having completed the recitation of the facts, the appellant in *Bell-Wesley v. O'Toole* might present his outline in the following manner:

> There are two parts to the argument that the Bell-Wesley's claim for damages should be recognized. First, Dr. O'Toole's behavior contains all the elements of standard medical malpractice. Second, recognizing an exception to standard tort law would contravene public policies favoring family planning and self-determination, discouragement of careless behavior, and the redress of harms.

The summary outline gives the judge a pattern into which to fit later arguments, indicates the order in which matters will be discussed, and enables the court to defer its questions until the appropriate time. Moreover, by announcing an outline near the beginning of your argument—even if in perfunctory form—you at least make the point that these particular arguments are important enough to be raised at oral argument. Even if lengthy questioning on an early point precludes discussing all of the topics on your outline, you may still summarize each point at the conclusion of the argument and ask the court for questions before you step down.

d. Making the point.

(1) *Presenting arguments.* At the preparation stage you determined which arguments were strongest, most important, and most persuasive. Make sure to put the best points to the court early in the argument. This both attracts the court's attention and ensures that the strongest points are not left out if you get sidetracked by questions. As a general rule, present arguments orally as you did in the brief, using an "inverted pyramid" structure. State conclusions first and then support them with facts and law. Setting out a series

of premises and then drawing conclusions is too complicated to be effective in oral argument.

(2) *Blending fact and law.* All arguments combine law and facts, and finding the appropriate mixture is something you will want to consider in organizing your presentation. Blending facts and law is essential because an argument that discourses on black-letter trends since Blackstone's era without mentioning their relevance to the parties in court, or one that describes the endlessly complex contract negotiations between the parties without alluding once to the legal implications of their dispute, is doomed to fail. Unless you integrate the factual and legal elements of your argument, no court will ever be able to understand your position or rule in your favor.

There is no formula for a perfectly blended argument. Because the relative proportions of fact and law differ in every case, developing this aspect of the advocate's art takes time and practice. You need to consider your own case closely. Are you asking the court to extend doctrine and create a new rule of law? If so, you may want to concentrate on legal arguments and explain why the existing rule has led to unfair results in prior cases. On the other hand, if you are merely asking the court to apply an established rule of law, you may want to spend more time on your facts.

You should be aware that some advocates believe the facts are all-important, that because any side of any case can be argued with flawless legal logic, the characterization of the facts will always carry the day. These practitioners tend to let their oral arguments encompass "facts" beyond the four corners of the record: reasonable inferences, social values and customs, political and economic theories, current events. When used expertly, this technique can be extremely effective. Remember, however, that you must be able to stride confidently through the relevant law, cases, and record thoroughly before you attempt any fancy footwork. Remember too that no court will tolerate a fabricated fact or a misrepresentation. Even a slight exaggeration is too much. If the record says "some" patrons of the casino were dancing on the craps table, don't tell the court that "most" of them were unless you are willing to invoke the judges' wrath.

e. Conclusion. Conclude your oral presentation by summarizing the most important arguments. This is particularly helpful if the court has broken up your arguments with questions. Explain to the court the relationship between each of your arguments, integrating them into an overall framework. Emphasize the strongest arguments in the conclusion.

When there is nothing left to say, thank the court and sit down— even if time is left. Any makeweight argument used to fill up the remaining time is likely to leave the court with an unfavorable impression and could seriously weaken those arguments already made.

2. The Appellee's Argument. Since the traditional appellee's argument is structurally similar to that of the appellant, the guidelines listed above will be helpful. If you represent the appellee, listen closely to appellant's argument and to the questions the judges ask. Take notes to remind yourself of points on which the judges dwell. You should have a tentative outline of your argument prepared but you should be ready to revamp and revise it on the spur of the moment in order to respond to issues that obviously concern the judges. You may also decide that something the appellant said during his presentation should be refuted or corrected. In short, be prepared to be spontaneous.

As a general rule, it is best to develop your own case rather than to attack your opponent's. However, on the points where the two sides directly disagree, you cannot avoid talking about the appellant's contentions. In these situations, aggressive respondents ("respondent" is synonomous with "appellee") may explicitly attack appellant's assertions. This affirmative method brings to the sharp and focused attention of the court the clear distinctions between the two parties.

3. Appellant's Rebuttal. At the beginning of the argument, the appellant may wish to reserve time for rebuttal. Rebuttal time should be used to clarify any prior arguments and react to the appellee's presentation. Because it is the court's last impression of the case, rebuttal can be very important. Avoid using numerous citations during the rebuttal.

Because time in the entire argument is limited, the reserved time should not be extensive. Appellant need use none of the reserved time, and in occasional circumstances one tactic would be to deny the need for rebuttal except to answer further questions. In any event, once appellant has made the points he wishes to make, the rebuttal should end.

C. QUESTIONS BY THE COURT

1. The Value of Questions. "Rejoice when the Court asks questions." [8] Questions from the court reveal to you what the judge is thinking. You finally learn whether the court understands your ideas, whether the judge agrees with your framing of the issues, and what troubles the judge.

Listening to the question makes the task of persuasion easier. If it is apparent from the nods of the judges or from their questions that they fully agree with the position taken on an issue, it may be a

---

[8] Davis, 26 A.B.A.J. at 897.

good idea to shorten the scheduled presentation and move on to a new area. If the questions indicate the court disagrees with certain contentions, it may be wise to amplify and present even more persuasively reasons that might convince the court of the position's validity. In short, questions allow the advocate to tailor the argument to the court's reaction.

Be aware at all times that not every question asked is an attack on your position; some questions are designed to support your view and some are simply points about which the judge is confused and has no preconceived opinion.

2. Effective Answering.

a. **Be responsive.** Using the court's own questions to persuade it of the soundness of a contention requires responsiveness on your part. To respond to questions adequately, you must understand what the judge has asked. Always listen carefully. If the question is unclear, you may properly ask the judge to repeat or rephrase it. If the implications of a question are unclear, you may repeat what you understand the judge to be asking and inquire whether that is what the judge means. You want to clarify your position and you need to clarify puzzling questions in order to do so. It is often wise to pause before you begin to speak to reflect briefly on the question. Taking a few seconds to collect your thoughts usually results in a more focused response. It is far more effective to pause and organize your response than to attempt one that is prompt, yet unclear.

A judge's questions may spring from confusion, misunderstanding, concern about the consequences of broadening a legal rule, hostility born of a personal conviction that your position is wrong, or a genuine desire to help you regain your footing after tough interrogation from a less than friendly colleague. You need to listen closely to questions to ascertain what troubles a judge and why. Your answers must explain and clarify your position until you satisfy the judge; if you try to move on without meeting her concerns, she will badger you until you do. If the judge believes you are being evasive, she may grow exasperated and simply decide to rule against you. Always be respectful, courteous, and above all, responsive. Under no circumstances should you tell a judge that you will get to her question later, when you have finished the point you are making. You must tailor your tentative schedule to fit the judges' interests, and an unwillingness to answer a question when put signals disrespect.

Recognize and accept helpful questions from a judge; these types of questions often come when another member of the panel is questioning the speaker intensively. Inexperienced counsel have more than once refused an argument set out on a silver platter by a judge who restated counsel's argument in a new way or supported his position with a new argument.

Be prepared to answer the hardest questions, since the court's decision will often turn on them. Answering the question put, rather than some other question, is one hallmark of a fine advocate. Almost any question can be anticipated and hence answered by the lawyer who takes the time to think through the problems and implications of his case. At the same time, you must remember that a judge's question may not be the one you anticipated. Tailor your answer accordingly; a judge likes to think that her question is unique and will probably resent what sounds like a "pat" answer.

b. Advocate. Use your responses to advance your argument, even if that means departing from the order your outline sets out. Once the court seems satisfied with an answer, try to make a smooth transition from that response to another, related topic. Your argument will be more effective if it flows naturally from one point to another. Do all you can to maintain the argument's continuity and avoid a moment of awkward silence when the judges have concluded a line of questioning and await your next set of points.

Using a question as a vehicle to advance a line of argument is not an easy skill to learn, but here is an example of how someone arguing for the appellant in *Bell-Wesley v. O'Toole* might go about it. If a judge asked, "Why didn't the Bell-Wesleys give the child up for adoption?", the appellants' attorney might answer:

> 1. Your honor, it may seem logical merely to give up the child for adoption and thus mitigate any of the expenses associated with the child which are requested in this action as damages. 2. However, the courts, and indeed society, recognize the special relationship created between a parent and child. Very rarely do we ever ask a parent to give up a child. And this occurs only when the parents are incapable of caring for the child. 3. Indeed, your honor, it is because of this social and moral ethic which links a child to his or her natural parents that there are substantial damages in this action. A child, while unexpected, should and must not be taken away. Nevertheless, the unexpected costs associated with the child incurred through negligence should be borne by Dr. O'Toole, the perpetrator of the negligent acts.

Part 1 of the sample answer restates the question. By restating the question counsel has shown that she fully understands the question asked. (Indeed, the judge could have interrupted and corrected any misperception of the question.) Moreover, she has also used the opportunity to add the context of damages to an otherwise open-ended and unmanageable question regarding adoption. This move takes a step toward creating not just a responsive answer, but one which affirmatively advances the argument. In Part 2, counsel has directly responded to the question. In Part 3, she uses the question and answer as a platform to advance her argument that extensive damages ought to be awarded. The attorney moves from a responsive position ("The Bell-Wesleys shouldn't have to give the child up for adoption, because . . ."), to an affirmative one ("Because the child shouldn't be given up for adoption, therefore . . .").

Good preparation is the key to answering questions. Although you may feel unprepared and apprehensive going into your first oral argument, you will probably be pleasantly surprised at how much you actually know and how well you do. One final point: if you truly cannot think of an answer, be very honest with the court. Being evasive is more detrimental than simply saying, "I don't know."

3. Particular Types of Questions Judges Might Ask

a. Questions seeking information about the facts. If the statement of facts is adequate and gives the court some idea of which facts were crucial, many time-consuming questions may be avoided. If factual items are central, a judge will often want to read them directly from the record. Consequently, you should be prepared to answer such questions with a reference to the page in the record where the fact can be found. It is important to know the possible relevance of facts that are absent from the record.

Questions about the facts may also come from the judge who feels that you have wandered too far from the facts of the case into an abstract discourse on the law. You may well want to "react" to the questions by sticking a little more closely in the argument to the case's factual setting. This also involves wording arguments to bring out the facts of the case. For instance, in making an argument concerning plaintiff's reliance on a statement by the defendant, counsel might say, "Mr. Goldstein relied on Ms. Wolfe's statement that the shipment of volleyballs arrived on time," rather than dryly saying, "Reliance by the plaintiff is indicated in this case."

b. Questions about "policy considerations". Questions of this nature are often phrased like this: "Counsel, would you comment upon . . .." Here the court wants to hear a fuller exposition of the factors that counsel deems relevant to a decision, and possibly a countering of opposing policy considerations. The question will usually point up something that is troubling the judge. The advocate's job is to find ways to recast and supplement points covered in the briefs, as well as to emphasize to the court the relative weight attributable to the factors advanced by both sides.

Sometimes, questions of this sort are phrased more argumentatively: "But, counsel, isn't it clear that . . .." The form of the question does not mean that the judge has necessarily decided against the position advanced. It may well be that his thinking is currently adverse to that position, yet you should not give up but rather try to put the point in a new light and use the utmost persuasion to change his mind. If it becomes clear that the judge is simply stating good law, you may well want to admit the validity of the judge's comment and direct the discussion to new ground.

c. Questions directed at the authorities cited. When a judge asks about a cited case, he wants something more than a dry recitation of the facts and the holding. He wants to know how it relates to the case being argued. Does it constitute binding precedent on the point (not likely in a mythical jurisdiction where every issue is one of first impression), or does it show the existing framework of law into which the desired result must be fitted? Above all, the judge wants to know why the earlier court decided as it did. What considerations did it think controlling? Has the weight to be given these factors changed since the court decided the earlier case? The advice of Justice Schaefer is relevant:

> Do not argue your case . . . in terms of rules. The law does not live in the statements of rule, including past statements of the rule by the court, any more than it lives in the black letter of the hornbook. The law lives and cases are decided . . . in that area of policy and in the considerations out of which the black-letter rules evolve . . . .. Keep your . . . argument pitched to take account of these considerations—not ostentatiously, I am sure I do not have to tell you that—but do not put your argument solely in terms of a bare absolute rule which the court may have announced in a particular case.[9]

You may sometimes have to argue against what seems to be established precedent. If this is the case, a frontal attack is usually appropriate. However, the precedent may actually be inapposite in the circumstances of the case before the court. When overturning established precedent is likely to be the primary subject for conversation between you and the judges, the following questions may be important:

(1) Is the precedent grounded on sound public policy?

(2) Is the precedent working well or badly in practice?

(3) Is the precedent being followed universally?

(4) Will the precedent become less useful in the future?

(5) Will the precedent create injustice in this particular case?

(6) Is the precedent consistent with trends in allied fields?

---

[9] W. Schaefer, 3 U. Chi. L. Sch. Rec. 1, 12 (No. 2, 1954).

(7) Can a valid and consistent exception to the precedent be made without detracting from the force of the precedent as a whole?[10]

d. Questions directed at particular legal arguments. Questions of this type test an argument's logic. Loose statements of holdings, overbroad analogies, and imprecise wording can unleash a veritable barrage of questions.

There remain questions directed at legal arguments, questions that legitimately spring from the arguments' complexity or implications. These questions test your mastery of the case and depth of understanding of the surrounding law. Judges often want to know how far an argument will take the court down an uncharted path. "Where will it end?" The question requires line drawing, yet this is precisely where the court needs guidance. If a judge is persuaded that a distinction can be drawn between the case at bar and a future case where the doctrine espoused seems applicable but where the result is untenable, then he is well on the way to adopting a favorable result. If you want to prevent the application of the doctrine espoused, be prepared to deliver what is often called a "parade of horribles," the negative implications of accepting opposing counsel's line of argument. Think through the implications of doctrines advocated by your opponent in order to be ready to offer responsive answers that may help the court decide the case.

Keep in mind that the case being argued involves specific parties in a single fact situation. If you weave the facts neatly into your answers, you can probably avoid getting trapped into defending a broad general principle against all possible attacks.

4. Questioning in team situations. Although judges in moot court competition will ordinarily refrain from questioning one member of the team about issues for which the other member was primarily responsible, it is advisable for each co-counsel to understand the basic arguments of the case. If questioning becomes too specific, ask the court either to permit your co-counsel to return to the lectern or, if you are the first oralist, to await your teammate's later appearance.

If properly prepared, the second speaker may also take the opportunity to cover crucial points that his co-counsel inadvertently omitted and to develop further any answers that may have been inadequate.

D. PRESENTING THE ORAL ARGUMENT

1. Be Yourself. If there is one general rule of presenting an argument, it is "Be yourself." If you are ordinarily even-tempered

[10] F. Kenison, "Some Aspects of Appellate Arguments," 1 N.H.B.J. 5, 12 (January 1959).

and soft spoken, don't plan to impress the court with a flashy, fist-pounding display of rhetoric. Don't try to fit yourself into someone else's mold. There is no single right way to argue a case, and the more comfortable you are, the more effective your argument is likely to be.

2. Effective Delivery. Read only if absolutely necessary. A paper barrier between court and counsel inhibits effective presentation. The best advocates have a thorough knowledge of relevant materials. This does not mean that an appellate lawyer becomes primarily a case-citer. Rather, she can deal quickly and surely with the issues, calling forth relevant arguments without fumbling through a mound of written materials for that case which is "here somewhere," or which "I saw just a moment ago." Eye contact with the judges is very important and can only be maintained when counsel has acquired a thorough knowledge of the material she will use in argument.

Quoting cases to support your arguments is sometimes useful, but keep the quotes short and do not use them too often. In general, paraphrasing the language of cases you cited in your brief will be a more effective way of communicating their essence to the judges.

Apply fundamentals of good public speaking. Don't orate; an appellate court is not a jury. "The play on an appellate court's emotions must be subtle and restrained if it is to be effective."[11] Oral argument comprehends discussion between court and counsel as well as mere address to the court. The whole is not a contest but a cooperative venture, a means to a contest's resolution. It is conversation as well as lecture, more dialogue than monologue. It is talking to and talking with. In court, a calm voice of reason persuades.

Some points of public speaking to keep in mind are:

a. Be heard.

b. Use proper emphasis. Avoid a ministerial cadence (sing-song) where the voice goes up and down without emphasizing the proper words.

c. Avoid mumbling.

d. Use the pause. This device, when used sparingly and judiciously, serves to stress the points being made and helps to regain a judge's attention when he has become preoccupied with a cited passage in the record or brief.

e. Maintain eye contact—don't read.[12]

[11] F. Wiener, "Oral Advocacy," 62   [12] Wiener, 62 Harv. L. Rev. at 60–64.
Harv. L. Rev. 56, 61 (1948).

3. What to Take to Court. Given the limited amount of time allotted for oral argument and the need for continuous presentation and dialogue, reference to materials may be limited. Proper preparation, including anticipating questions to be asked, reduces the need to search through materials for one's answers.

Take the record and briefs with you to the lectern. The court is more than likely to ask questions that specifically refer to these documents. (Make sure that you tab or clip pertinent pages in the record and briefs so that you can refer to them effortlessly should the need arise.) Three other kinds of materials may be helpful. First, a short outline of points to be covered serves as a helpful checklist to jog your memory. Second, note cards containing important facts and quotations may be useful. You can write key words pertaining to particular points or cases on separate cards, which can be shuffled discreetly during your presentation. Finally, several blank sheets of paper are invaluable for taking notes during your opponent's or your teammate's argument about questions the judges are asking or points you realize you must make.

4. Attitude Toward the Court. Your attitude toward the court should be one of respectful intellectual equality. You are not servile to the court, but you must accord judges due respect. Irritated people are not easily persuaded. Even in the heat of hard questioning, you must take care to be receptive, cooperative and in no way show annoyance at the trend of the questioning. Give definite answers to the court's questions and be aggressive with the material even as you avoid being aggressive in manner.

5. Handling Miscitations and Misrepresentations by Opposing Counsel. Bring any miscitations and misrepresentations of opposing counsel to the court's attention only if you feel they are important to the case. In evaluating their importance, you should determine whether they may be influencing an essential argument, or whether, without help, the court will be unable to find the appropriate citation. In addition, it is important to evaluate whether the court realizes that the material has been misrepresented. Be careful not to appear to be attacking opposing counsel personally.

6. Formal Conduct. A few customs of formal conduct should be observed in the oral argument. The customs do not vary much from courtroom to courtroom. When beginning the argument, rise and say, "May it please the court," or "If the court please," and introduce yourself. In answering questions, address the judge as "Your Honor." In referring to members of the court, "Judge Smith" or "The Chief Justice" is appropriate. Opposing counsel should be referred to as such, or as "Ms. Overton" or "counsel for the defendant" but never as "my opponent." Associate counsel is called "my colleague," "my associate," or "Ms. Phethean."

INDEX

References are to Pages

ABBREVIATIONS
Case names, 113.
General style, 98.
State names, 116.

ADMISSIONS
By party-opponent, 5.
Use of in statement of facts, 42.

ANSWER
Sample, 15–16.

AUTHORITIES
See also Legal Sources.
Choosing, 29–30, 46.
Comparing, 26–28, 47.
Function of, 46.
Identification of, see Citations.
Opposing, 47
    Citation to, 106–107.
Order, 105, 107.
Parentheticals used to explain, 46, 110–111.
Relative importance, 26, 46.

BRIEF
Generally, 37–39.
Argument formulation for, 6–9, 44–45.
Authority, use of within, 46.
    See also Authorities.
Editing, 48–49.
Oral advocacy, comparison with, 37, 124.
Preemption and rebuttal within, 45.
Sample briefs, 51, 75.
Sections,
    Argument headings, 44.
      Samples, 60, 83.
    Arguments, 44–46.
    Citations, Table of, 48, 102.
      Samples, 55–56, 79–80.
    Conclusion, 46.
      Samples, 73, 97.
    Introduction, 41.
    Questions presented, 39–41.
      Samples, 40–41.
    Statement of Facts, 41–44.
      See also Facts.
    Table of Contents, 48.
      Samples, 53, 77.

BRIEF—Cont'd
    Title page, 47.
      Samples, 51, 75.
Stylistic guidelines, 37–39.
Tone, 38, 50.

CAPITALIZATION
Generally, 99.

CASES
    See also Authorities; Citations.
Abbreviations in case names, 113.
Citation of, 111–118.
Use of as precedent, 29, 46.

CITATIONS
Abbreviations, 98.
Annotated Reports System, 117.
Briefs, 123.
Cases, 111–118.
Citation sentences, 105, 108.
Comparing authorities, 107.
Concurring opinions, 110.
Constitutions, 121.
Court, 104.
Date, 104.
Dicta, 110.
Dissenting opinions, 110.
Encyclopedias, 123.
English statutes, 121.
Federal cases, 113–115.
Federal statutes, 119.
Incomplete, 115, 118.
Indication of purpose and weight, 105–111.
Internal revenue code, 120.
Law reviews, 122.
Necessary elements, 103–105.
Newspapers, 123.
Omissions in case names, 112.
Parentheticals indicating weight and explanation, 46–47, 110–111.
Recent reports, 115, 118.
Record, reference to, 42.
    Samples of, 58, 82.
Restatements, 121.
Rules of procedure, 120.
Session laws and compilations, 118.
Signals indicating purpose, 105–107.
    See also Signals.

143

CITATIONS—Cont'd
Spacing, 103.
State cases, 116–118.
State statutes, 120.
Statutes, 118–121.
Subsequent and prior history, 112.
Treatises, 121.
Uniform Acts, 120.

COMPLAINT
Sample, 11–13.

CORE THEORY
Development and use of,
In brief writing, 8.
In oral argument, 126.

COURTS
Findings of fact by, 5.
Sample, 17.
Judgment, sample, 22.
Moot court, peculiarities of, 1–3.
Opinion, sample, 20.

ETHICAL CONSIDERATIONS
Adverse facts, use of, 43.
Citation of decisions contra, 47, 106.
Miscitations and misrepresentations by
opposing counsel, 142.
Record, reliance on in appellate advocacy,
4, 42.

FACTS
Adverse facts, treatment of, 5, 43.
Findings of, 5.
Sample, 17.
Judicial notice of, 42.
Statement of facts,
In brief, 41–44.
Samples, 57, 81.
In oral argument, 132.
Use of in development of argument, 6–9,
42.

ITALICIZATION
Generally, 99–100.

LEGAL RESEARCH
See also Legal Sources.
Argument formulation before, 6–9.
Bridge sources, 27.
Case annotated research tools, 32.
Computer data bases, 35.
Headnotes, 32.
Key number system, West, 30–31.
Primary sources, 26, 29.
Secondary sources, 27.
Shepard's Citations, 33–35.
West's Reporter System, 30.

LEGAL SOURCES
American Jurisprudence, 28, 32, 123.
American Law Reports, 31, 123.
Case annotated research tools, 32.
Case digests, 31.
Corpus Juris Secundum, 28, 123.
Federal Reporter, 30, 31, 114.
General Digests, West's, 30.
Hornbooks, 27.
Indexes to legal articles, 29.
Law reviews, 27, 122.
Lawyer's Cooperative System, 31.
Legal encyclopedias, 27–28, 123.
Lexis, 35.
Official reporters, 113, 115, 116, 118.
Pocket parts, 28.
Regional reporters, 30, 117.
Restatements of the Law, 27, 121.
Shepard's Citation System, 33.
Specialty sources, 36.
Statutes, 32, 118–121.
Supreme Court Reporter, 113–114.
Treatises, 27, 121–122.
United States Code, 32, 119.
United States Reporter, 113.
Westlaw, 35.
West's Reporter System, 30.

NOTICE OF APPEAL
Sample, 23.

ORAL ARGUMENT
Appellant's argument, 128, 131, 135.
Appellee's argument, 128, 135.
Choice of arguments for, 126–127.
Conclusion, 134.
Conduct during, 136–137, 140–141.
Organization, 131.
Precedent, use and value of, 139.
Preparation, 125, 128–129.
Presentation, 133, 140–142.
Questions by the court, responding to,
135–140.
Rebuttal, 135.
Rehearsal, 130.
Statement of the facts within, 132.
Strategy, 127.
Styles, 127.

PARENTHETICALS
Explaining case and facts, 46–47, 111.
Indicating author, 111.
Indicating weight, 110.
Order of, 111.

QUOTATIONS
Alterations, 101.
Indication of page numbers, 101.
Length, 39, 100.
Omissions, 100–101.
Placement of quotations marks, 100.

QUOTATIONS—Cont'd
When indented, 102.

RECORD
Holes in, treatment of, 42.
How to examine, 4.
Inferring facts from, 5, 42.
Issue determination, 5–6.
Judicial notice, use of, 42.
Legal research, use of record to facili-
 tate, 9.
References to, 42.
 Samples, 58, 82.
Relative weight of sources within, 5.
Statement of facts, use of record to de-
 velop, 5, 42.

REFERENCES
 See also Citations.
Briefs, 123.
"Ibid", 102.
"Infra", 102.
Record, 42.
"Supra", 102.

SIGNALS
 Generally, 47, 105.
"Accord," 106.

SIGNALS—Cont'd
"But cf.", 107.
"But see", 107.
"Cf.", 106.
"Contra," 106.
"E.g.," 106.
Order of, 107.
Order within, 108.
"See", 106.

STATUTES
Annotated, 32.
Citation to, 118–121.

STYLE
Abbreviations, 98.
Capitalization, 99.
Delivery style in oral argument, 127.
Italicization, 99.
Numbers, symbols, and dates, 100.
Spacing of citations, 103.
Technical words of reference, 102.
Writing style, 37.

TABLE OF CITATIONS
 Generally, 48.
Rules of style, 102.
Samples, 55–56, 79–80.

†

0-88277-249